Cover photography by Tony Szuta

TABLE OF CONTENTS

acknowledgments

Ever pick up a book and find that, once again, the author has dedicated a book to someone else, and not you? Granted, there's not a thing wrong with that. Spouses and family members in general are often the inspiration behind writers to "do their thing." But...not this time.

No, this time, this particular publication is dedicated to the plethora of Hot Wheels collectors out there who have kept this hobby alive and well since Redlines first graced the public back in the late-60's. We're a dedicated bunch for sure, with our tubs of sealed Hot Wheels in those Rubbermaid bins or boxes, and our mancave (or girlcave?) walls covered with Hot Wheels still on the card, or in display cabinets. Or even all those loose cars that we keep in a mountain of cases. We're completists. Aficionados. Collectors with insane attention to detail. But, mostly, we're a part of a huge contingency that loves its small toy cars. It's a love affair that for many of us dates back to our childhood, when we were slinging these little cars around in the dirt, or running them down orange tracks at breakneck speed. Or, maybe you were like me, and loved to inflict "real life" damage by cramming a Black Cat firecracker into the windows, and lighting it up. Or hurtling them toward each other for insane head-on collisions. Yeah, I'm admitting to that. My Hot Wheels were played with...I didn't have the discipline or desire to keep them in the package.

I've been humbled to be a part of this hobby since I returned to it in 1995. Think about all that's changed, just since then. The Internet was in its infancy, but I still managed to get a Hot Wheels website up on Geocities by 1998. I never dreamed the website would evolve into the database that it's become, and that it would be closing in on 20 million hits, even despite being shut down for the better part of 5 years before the re-launch.

So, I'm dedicating this publication to the collectors. You've all inspired me to maintain the NCHWA.com website throughout all these years, even though it can be a bear, sometimes. It's been worth it. This is for YOU. But, I'd be remiss if I didn't also thank the following people who've been so awesome throughout the years:

Elliot Handler, Mattel Founder: For sticking to his guns, being right and taking on the mighty Matchbox! RIP.
Larry Wood & All past/present Hot Wheels Designers, for fueling childhood adventures and imaginations!
Amy Boylan, former "Chief" of HotWheelsCollectors.com for all of her support in the early days
Carson Lev, former Director of Engineering, Director of Design and Director of Hot Wheels Licensing
Wayne Scott, former designer/pinstriper extraordinaire at Mattel for his support at one of our shows
Mike Zarnock, for letting me bounce thoughts off him from time to time.
Dave Chang, Designer of the immortal KustomCity Evo, and one of the first websites I linked to back in the late 90's
The K*Mart 7: Members who started the NCHWA as a club with me on that frigid day in February, 1998. RIP, Jack.
Mom & Dad, for buying me all those Hot Wheels back in the late 70's, crazy 80's.
My Kids, Carson, Cherie and Anthony for growing up in this hobby...pretty much with me! ;)
Joe and Vinny Garceau, my buddies in crime, growing up. Lord, forgive us for all we did. We were just kids.
Jennifer Walter, despite all of the eye-rolling and general disdain for Hot Wheels...for still loving me!
Justin Edwards & Family: I couldn't ask for a better best friend or "adopted family!"
All Former NCHWA Club Members, from back in the day. It was an absolute BLAST!

Also, a shout-out to all of the folks who keep up with some of those amazing Hot Wheels websites out there. I know how much work it can be, and it's great that we have multiple resources on the Internet for our hobby. Last, but not least...a huge shout-out to all of the collectors who have emailed me with feedback, questions and suggestions. Your input is not only vital...but appreciated. Thank you, all.

~Neal Giordano

FORWARD

In my opinion, Hot Wheels history can pretty much be divided into 4 generations of classification: The Redline era, which spanned the late-60's to the late 70's. The Blackwall Era, which ran from the late-70's to early 90's. The Blue Card/Collector Numbers Era, which ran from 1989-1994. And, the present Era...which really has no name, so I'll call it: The Treasure Hunt Era. Applicable? A matter of opinion, to be sure. But, when you think about it, what other segment of cars has had more impact in our modern age of collecting, since 1995?

From their inception, collectors knew these cars were special. Aiding the 1995 hype was the fact that the Limited run number of 10K per car was printed on the blistercard. Values for each car quickly approached 3 figures and more, and they became nearly impossible to find (unless a collector had an inside edge, luck, or just plain scads of disposable income). To this day, the 1995 Treasure Hunt line is still easily the most valuable. Granted, many of the cars have gone well below the $100 line, but they still sell very briskly and profitably on the secondary market. The "Holy Grail" of all Treasure Hunts came from the 1995 line: The '67 Camaro. You wouldn't think that a rather ordinary-looking enamel white car with orange stripes, orange interior and chrome hub Real Rider tires would generate so much excitement...but, it did. The car now easily averages more than $350 on eBay, sometimes exceeding $400. Why is this the case? Simply put, the '67 Camaro, despite its seemingly overproduced state, remains one of the most popular Hot Wheels castings today. This may be an homage back to the original "Sweet 16" 1968 Hot Wheels, where the Custom Camaro was one of the more popular models. The casting was modified in later releases, but it still captures the essence of its vintage 1:1 version.

1996 Treasure Hunts were received almost as enthusiastically, and the values mirrored the 1995 releases at least for a short time. Those values would drop, however, as everyone understood that there were 15K more of the 1996 releases versus the 1995's. As most are aware, the 1995 TH line was limited to a release of 10K per car. In 1996, this would increase to 25K. From 1997 to present day, Mattel refuses to release the run numbers. None of us can even make an educated guess as to present day numbers, to be honest.

A good number of collectors consider the essence of a Treasure Hunt to be in the wheels. Real Riders, to many, define the true definition of a Limited Edition car. So, you can imagine the dismay of collectors when the 1997 Treasure Hunt line was released...WITHOUT Real Riders. Collectors were instantly up in arms about this change, and the resale values quickly reflected that dissatisfaction; secondary prices would never even remotely approach the values of the 1995 and 1996 lines. Also contributing to the low values was the casting selection. Uninspiring models such as the Blimp, Dogfighter and Buick Wildcat certainly weren't sending pulses racing.

The "Real Rider-less" and odd casting selection issue would continue through the 1998 and 1999 lines. Thankfully, the 2000 line reintroduced Real Riders, and collectors were once again enthusiastic about Treasure Hunts.

The 2000-2006 lines were par for the course, with some interesting (and some not-so interesting) models released. There are many gems within those lines, and their value on the secondary is reflected as such.

The 2007 Treasure Hunt line brought major changes, where a 2-tier system was introduced. Each Treasure Hunt would now have a "Regular" version, and what came to be known as a "Super" version. The "Regs" would have standard plastic wheels and normal paint jobs, while the "Supers" were issued with metallic/Spectraflame paints and Real Riders. Regulars and Supers would still share the same deco scheme. The values for the Supers shot through the roof, especially upon their release. They sold for unbelievable prices, as the "Gotta-have-it-itus" syndrome ran wild. Those values would drop as time went on, but the Supers were generating incredible collector response, and the values reflected that. The Regs would sell well, but their values obviously never even remotely approached those of their counterparts.

The 2-tier system of the same car having a Regular and Super version would continue through 2011, but changes were on the way. 2012 ushered in the practice of completely separating the Regulars from the Supers by utilizing different castings. Regulars would continue to have standard paint jobs and plastic wheels, and Supers would also continue with premium paint and wheels, but there would be no "twin" Regular Treasure Hunts. But, there was another major change: The Supers were now "hidden" within the line, and the blistercards were standard, with NO Treasure Hunt markings! The names "Hidden TH" or "Secret TH" began to circulate among collectors. There was one inherent problem with the new Super: A picture of the first one to be released began making its way around the Internet before it was released, and many were confused, or calling it a fake. That auspicious honor fell to the '69 Dodge Coronet:

The confusion and suspicion of the Coronet being a fake/custom was due to the car "looking like a Super," but being mounted on a normal-looking blister. This was before collectors found out about the impending "hidden Super" concept. Many discounted it as a custom, but others insisted on its authenticity due to the little "TH" logo on the front quarter panel. Shortly after, Mattel confirmed the process on HotWheelsCollectors.com, and values for the hidden Supers took off.

In 2013, the beloved "Green Stripe" that indicated the car was a Regular Treasure Hunt was dropped. And, to further complicate the process, Supers and Regs were hidden within the line, forcing collectors to really scan the pegs to find them. The only indicator that a car was a Regular (the Supers stood out on their own, and were completely unmistakable, even without the green stripe!) was a tiny circle flame logo hidden somewhere within the deco, and some text behind the car that could possibly not even be seen at all, depending on the size of the model (yes, that's a spelling error you see on the word "let's"....it still has yet to be changed:

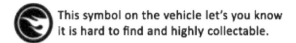

This symbol on the vehicle let's you know
It is hard to find and highly collectable.

This new release system for Treasure Hunts definitely sent a ripple of uncertainty throughout the Hot Wheels community. Many weren't even aware that the little flame circle logo indicated a Regular TH for MONTHS after the fact! To make matters worse, collectors scouring the pegs would get a TH rush when they spotted that oh-so-familiar "green stripe" on the blister card, only to find out that it was…just another segment, and not a TH. It took awhile for many collectors to adjust to this, but the process is understood by most, now.

Another issue that caused confusion with the Regulars now using the flame logo was the fact that some other cars in the line would also utilize the same logo within the deco scheme. Many of these ended up on eBay, touted as Treasure Hunts, but this wasn't the case.

So, here we are now, in 2015. The hidden concept for Regulars and Supers that was established in 2012 still carries over today. Whether the system stays in place remains to be seen…Mattel hasn't hesitated to throw a wrench into the works over the last decade or so…you just never know! Until then, the Treasure Hunt line will continue to create excitement, controversy and general misinformation from time to time, but hey…that's our hobby!

about this Guide

What you now hold in your hands is a Treasure Hunt Guide that guarantees each model from 1995-2014 has been meticulously researched with a MINIMUM 12-sample average. Yes, there are going to be auctions where a particular model will go WELL OVER or even under the values quoted here. Average values don't account for all-out bidding skirmishes that take place among feverish collectors who insist on winning that model at any cost, or auctions that go unnoticed, due to poor verbiage. What I've done is take 12 auctions, high and low, and averaged them out to attain the value on the car. So, you may not have that skyrocketing value you're hoping for, but what you DO have is a solid *average* value that each car is currently selling for. The values reflected within will give you a very good idea of your buy/sell margins.

You may be wondering why I didn't include the 2015 models... to me, it doesn't make sense to include the current year in this guide, simply due to the fact that the TH's are too "new", and value/perceived value doesn't tend to settle down until a year after their release. 2015 will be included in Vol. II, which is slated for release around May, 2016.

I'm often asked when the best time to sell your Treasure Hunts exists. To that, I'll answer "Right away, upon release." The vast majority of Super TH's have the most value when only a few folks have them. The values they'll attain on eBay or other secondary markets will unlikely EVER match what they're valued at when they're new. Collectors have to have them...and many will pay exorbitant amounts to win them in auctions. Now, I've never understood this, as the values are entirely guaranteed to decline...sometimes, quite a bit, depending on the model. The reality is, current releases (with only rare exceptions) of Treasure Hunts will never match the heyday of the 1995 issues as far as value goes. It's just not going to happen. Yes, newly-released Supers can attain tremendous returns on the secondary, but I can promise you that those values are going to deflate...and fairly quickly, once the "newness" wears off. A Super that garnered $80 on eBay will soon be selling in the mid-$20's or less, not long after. As collectors, we've all seen this. Some will pay INSANE amounts even for the new Regulars when they first come out, sometimes exceeding $30! Then, reality sets in when the value inevitably drops. Regulars are a nice concept, but they simply don't garner much more than standard Mainline releases, when it's all said and done.

Others may look at the values listed within and say: "That's it?" A collector may think Treasure Hunts are going to break the bank, but if you're looking at these from an investment standpoint, well...you may be disappointed. If you're a non-believer, then I invite you to go ahead and do what I've already done here: Pick a TH on eBay, take the last 10 auctions and average it out. I guarantee you'll find a similar value here in the guide.

Lastly, no matter what, there is never going to be a "bible" for Hot Wheels values, regardless of technique. We can always get a target value, but nothing's ever exact. There will always be fluctuations in the hobby that affect values. That being said, I do believe that averaging out recent sales is a very good indicator of potential value, and I think this method will present itself well in this Guide. It's the same method I use for the price guide at NCHWA.com.

I wish you all the best with your collecting, and I'd like to thank you for purchasing the guide.

Neal Giordano

Neal Giordano
Founder/Editor, North Carolina Hot Wheels Association
Website: www.nchwa.com
Email: nchwa@yahoo.com

1995

The first year for Treasure Hunts were limited to a run of 10K per model. Most of the models in 1995 exceeded the $100 mark on the secondary, but the values soon settled in to their present level. The most valuable models in the 1995 segment are the '67 Camaro, with 3 known variations, and the VW Bug, which still sells for more than $100. The least valuable model is the Classic Caddy.

Card #	Name	Description	Value
353	Olds 442	Metalflake blue body with chrome Malaysia base and Redline Real Riders	68
354	Gold Passion	Metalflake gold body with black HW logo, Malaysia base and Real Riders	63
354	Gold Passion	Same as original, but with pink/black HW logo	115
355	'67 Camaro	White body with orange stripes, Malaysia base and grey hub Real Riders	364
355	'67 Camaro	Same as original, but with chrome hub rear wheels	1,142
355	'67 Camaro	Same as original, but without HW logo on rear window	610
356	'57 T-Bird	Metalflake purple body with Malaysia base and Whiteline Real Riders	53
357	VW Bug	Bright green body with Malaysia base and purple Turbo wheels	125
358	'63 Split Window	Metalflake blue body with Malaysia base and Whiteline Real Riders	72
359	Stutz Blackhawk	Metalflake black body with Malaysia base and Redline Real Riders	48
360	Rolls Royce	Burgundy body with Malaysia base and chrome/red 6-Spoke/Pro Circuits	50
361	Classic Caddy	Green body/fenders, Malaysia base and gold 6-Spoke/Pro Circuit wheels	43
362	Classic Nomad	Metalflake teal body with Malaysia base and chrome Swirl wheels	60
363	Classic Cobra	Green body with gold stripes, Malaysia base and gold 6-Spoke/Pro Circuits	82
364	'31 Doozie	Yellow /black body with Malaysia base and yellow 6-Spoke/Pro Circuits	45
N/A	12-Car TH Set	J.C. Penny Box Set, Limited Edition (1 of 2,000)	1,369

Expected **Average** Cost to acquire the 1995 set car by car, individually (excluding variations): **$1,073**

1996

1996 Treasure Hunts were limited to 25K per model, and continued the trend of great models and Real Riders. The most valuable models in the 1996 segment are the '40's Woodie variations and the Lamborghini Countach. The least valuable model is the Jaguar XJ220. An insane error was also issued in '96: A red Dodge Viper, which was supposed to be a Mainline car, was accidentally issued on a Treasure Hunt card. The real Viper TH was white with Real Riders. The red Viper is NOT considered rare, and garners far less than the white version. Great conversation piece, though!

Card #	Name	Description	Value
428	40's Woodie	Yellow body with Malaysia base and yellow hubs with Yellowline Real Riders	16
428	40's Woodie	Same as original, but with silver rims on the wheels	39
428	40's Woodie	Same as original, but with gold rims on the wheels	54
429	Lamborghini	Bright orange body with Malaysia base and 6-Spoke Pro Circuit wheels	30
429	Lamborghini	Same as original, but with 5-Spoke wheels	80
430	Ferrari 250	Metalflake grey body with Malaysia base and chrome hub Real Rider tires	16
431	Jaguar XJ220	Metalflake green body with Malaysia base and gold Pro Circuit 6-Spoke tires	12
432	'59 Caddy	Red body with Malaysia base and chrome hub Whiteline Real Rider tires	15
433	Dodge Viper	White body with blue stripes and white hub Pro Circuit 6-Spoke tires	17
210	Dodge Viper	Red body with black chassis and Lace wheels (Mainline error/mis-package)	5
434	'57 Chevy	Purple body with Malaysia base and chrome hub GoodYear Real Rider tires	24
435	Ferrari 355	White body with Malaysia base and gold 5-Spoke Pro Circuit tires	19
436	'58 Corvette	Metalflake teal body with Malaysia base and chrome Swirl wheels	19
437	Auburn 852	Metalflake gold body with Malaysia base and gold hub Real Rider tires	13
438	Dodge Ram	Metalflake red body with Malaysia base and chrome hub Real Rider tires	15
439	'37 Bugatti	Metalflake blue body with Malaysia base and chrome 6-Spoke Pro Circuit tires	14
N/A	12-Car TH Set	J.C. Penny Box Set, Limited Edition (1 of 5,000)	192

Expected **Average** Cost to acquire the 1996 set car by car, individually (excluding variations): **$210.00**

1997

1997 Treasure Hunts marked the first year Mattel didn't release run numbers on the series, and introduced the elimination of Real Riders. The most valuable models in the 1997 segment are the Rail Rodder and the Hot Rod Wagon. The least valuable model is the Avus Quattro. Values dropped steeply during this release year.

Card #	Name	Description	Value
578	'56 Flashsider	Metalflake green body with Malaysia base and 5-Spoke tires	7
579	Silhouette II	Enamel white body with Malaysia base and white hub 3-Spoke tires	5
580	Mercedes 500SL	Black body with Malaysia base and 5-Spoke tires	5
581	Street Cleaver	Black body with Malaysia base, gold metal plow and 5-Spoke tires	6
582	GM Lean Machine	Metalflake burgundy body with Malaysia base and 5-Spoke tires	5
583	Hot Rod Wagon	Yellow body with Malaysia base and yellow hub 5-Spoke tires	11
584	Olds Aurora	Metalflake purple body with Malaysia base and 5-Spoke tires	5
585	Dogfighter	Metalflake green body with yellow Malaysia base and 5-Spoke tires	7
586	Buick Wildcat	Metalflake silver body with grey Malaysia base and 3-Spoke tires	7
587	Blimp	Blue body with Malaysia base and white gondola	6
588	Avus Quattro	Metalflake gold body with black Malaysia base and Sawblade wheels	4
589	Rail Rodder	White body with metal Malaysia base and Micro wheels on front	13
N/A	12-Car TH Set	J.C. Penny Box Set, Limited Edition (1 of 5,000)	113

Expected **Average** Cost to acquire the 1997 set car by car, individually (no variations): **$81.00**

1998

The most valuable models in the 1998 segment are the Kenworth and the Scorchin' Scooter. The least valuable model is the Turbo Flame. Values remained low during this release year.

Card #	Name	Description	Value
749	Twang Thang	Black body with blue chrome guitars, Malaysia base and 5-Spoke tires	4
750	Scorchin' Scooter	Red body with metal Malaysia base and 3-Spoke Motorcycle tires	9
751	Kenworth T600A	Purple body with chrome Malaysia base and 3-Spoke wheels	10
752	3-Window '34	Orange body with metal Malaysia base and 5-Hole wheels	7
753	Turbo Flame	Chrome green body with black metal Malaysia base and 5-Spoke wheels	3
754	Saltflat Racer	Black/gold body with gold metal Thailand base and 5-Spoke wheels	4
755	Street Beast	Red/white body with metal Malaysia base and gold Lace wheels	3
756	Road Rocket	Chrome/translucent body with metal Malaysia base and 3-Spoke wheels	3
757	Sol-Aire CX7	White body with blue Malaysia base and white Lace wheels	5
758	'57 Chevy	Metalflake green body with gold Thailand base and 3-Spoke wheels	5
759	Stingray III	Silver body with black Malaysia base and 3-Spoke wheels	3
760	Way 2 Fast	Metalflake dark green body with metal Thailand base and 5-Spoke wheels	5
N/A	12-Car TH Set	J.C. Penny Box Set, Limited Edition (1 of 5,000)	104

Expected **Average** Cost to acquire the 1998 set car by car, individually (no variations): **$61.00**

1999

The most valuable models in the 1999 segment are the Ferrari variations and the Mach I. The least valuable model is the Jaguar D-Type. Values remained low during this release year.

Card #	Name	Description	Value
929	Mercedes 540K	Red body, black interior, metal Malaysia chassis	4
930	T-Bird Stocker	Blue body, yellow interior, grey Malaysia chassis	4
931	'97 Corvette	Purple body, yellow interior, tinted windows, black Thailand chassis	4
932	Rigor Motor	Yellow body with black metal Malaysia chassis and gold 5-Spoke wheels	3
933	Ferrari 512M	Yellow body with metal Malaysia chassis and 5-Spoke Pro Circuit wheels	10
933	Ferrari 512M	Same as original, but with black painted base	26
933	Ferrari 512M	Same as original, but with 6-Spoke wheels	40
934	'59 Impala	Purple body, white interior, gold chrome Thailand chassis and gold Lace wheels	5
935	Hot Wheels 500	Black body, black interior, metal Malaysia chassis and black 7-Spoke wheels	4
936	Jaguar D-Type	Black body, black interior, metal Malaysia chassis and 5-Spoke wheels	2
937	'32 Ford Delivery	Gold body w/purple fenders, metal Malaysia chassis and gold 5-Spoke wheels	6
938	Hot Seat	Translucent body, metal Malaysia chassis and 5-Spoke wheels	4
939	Mustang Mach I	Green body, black interior, black Malaysia chassis and 5-Spoke wheels	12
940	Express Lane	Purple body, metal Malaysia chassis and gold 5-Spoke wheels	5
N/A	12-Car TH Set	J.C. Penny Box Set, Limited Edition (1 of 3,500)	97

Expected **Average** Cost to acquire the 1999 set car by car, individually (excluding variations): **$63.00**

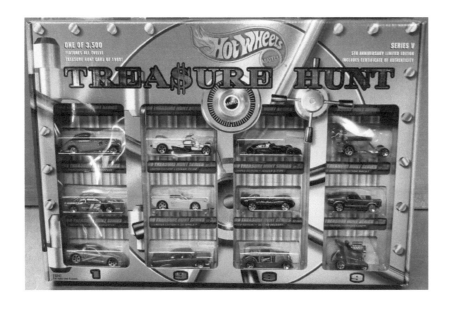

2000

The most valuable models in the 2000 segment are the Go Kart, Cord with whitewalls and the GTO. The least valuable model is the Lakester (shocking, I know!) Values remained low during this release year.

Card #	Name	Description	Value
49	Double Vision	Purple body with chrome Malaysia base and chrome hub Real Riders	3
50	Tow Jam	Yellow body with chrome Malaysia base and chrome hub Real Riders	3
51	1936 Cord	Silver body with chrome Malaysia base and chrome hub Real Riders	6
51	1936 Cord	Same as original, but with whitewall Real Riders	10
52	Sweet 16 II	Red body with metal Malaysia base and chrome hub Real Riders	3
53	Lakester	Green body with black metal Malaysia base and gold 5-Spoke wheels	2
54	Go Kart	White body with metal Malaysia base, gold RR on rear/Micro Wheels on front	10
55	Chaparral II	Blue body with white metal Malaysia base and chrome hub Real Riders	4
56	'57 T-Bird	Green body with chrome Malaysia base and chrome hub Real Riders	4
57	Pikes Peak Celica	Blue body with black plastic Malaysia base and gold Real Riders	5
57	Pikes Peak Celica	Same as original, but with chrome Real Riders	13
57	Pikes Peak Celica	Same as original, but with 3-Spoke wheels	30
58	'67 Pontiac GTO	White body with gold chrome Malaysia base and gold Real Riders	8
58	'67 Pontiac GTO	Same as original, but with Thailand base	8
59	Ford GT-40	Gold body with black Thailand base and chrome hub Real Riders	4
60	1970 Chevelle	Black body with chrome China or Malaysia base and chrome Real Riders	7
N/A	12-Car TH Set	J.C. Penny Box Set, Limited Edition (1 of 3,500)	100

Expected **Average** Cost to acquire the 2000 set car by car, individually (excluding variations): **$59.00**

2001

The most valuable models in the 2001 segment are the Charger and the Blast Lane. The least valuable model is the Hammered Coupe. Values remained low during this release year.

Card #	Name	Description	Value
001	'65 Corvette	Red body with Malaysia base and chrome hub Real Riders	5
002	Roll Cage	Orange cage with Malaysia base and GoodYear Off-Road chrome hub Real Riders	4
003	So Fine	Metalflake green body with Malaysia base and chrome hub Whitewall Real Riders	4
004	Rodger Dodger	Black body with Malaysia base and chrome hub Whitewall Real Riders	5
005	Blast Lane	Metalflake gold body with Malaysia base and gold 3-Spoke Motorcycle wheels	6
006	Hammered Coupe	Silver/black body with Malaysia base and PR5 wheels	2
007	Vulture	White body with translucent orange Malaysia base and PR5 wheels	2
008	'67 Charger	Yellow body with Malaysia base and chrome hub Real Riders	6
009	Olds 442	Metalflake blue body with Malaysia base and chrome hub Real Riders	4
010	Pontiac Rageous	Metalflake brown body with Malaysia base and chrome hub Real Riders	2
011	Deora	Metalflake blue body with Thailand base and repro Redline wheels	5
012	Cabbin' Fever	White body with gold Malaysia base and PR5 wheels	4
N/A	12-Car TH Set	J.C. Penny Box Set, Limited Edition (1 of 3,500)	92

Expected **Average** Cost to acquire the 2001 set car by car, individually (excluding variations): **$49.00**

2002

The most valuable models in the 2002 segment are the Mini Cooper and Plymouth GTX. The least valuable model is the '57 Roadster. Values remained low during this release year. 2002 would mark the last year that J.C. Penny would issue the 12-car set. Going forward, it would be released by HotWheelsCollectors.com.

Card #	Name	Description	Value
001	La Troca	Yellow body with gold Malaysia base and chrome hub Real Riders	4
002	Plymouth GTX	Yellow body with gold Malaysia base and chrome hub Real Riders	5
003	'57 Roadster	Green body with Malaysia base and 5-Spk front/chrome hub Real Riders on rear	2
003	'57 Roadster	Same as original, but with all 5-Spoke wheels	3
004	Lotus M250	Burgundy body with Malaysia base and chrome hub Redline Real Riders	3
005	Ford Thunderbolt	Metalflake silver body with Malaysia base and chrome hub Real Riders	4
006	Panoz LMP-1	White/blue body with Malaysia base and chrome hub Real Riders	2
007	Phaeton	White body with Malaysia base and chrome hub Whitewall Real Riders	3
008	F/Fendered '40	Flat-black body with Thailand base and chrome hub Real Riders	3
008	F/Fendered '40	Same as original, but with semi-gloss black paint	6
009	'40 Ford Truck	Aqua/white body with Thailand base and chrome hub Real Riders	5
010	Tail Dragger	Purple body with Malaysia base and chrome hub Real Riders	3
011	Mini Cooper	Black body with painted headlights, Malaysia base and Redline Real Riders	18
011	Mini Cooper	Same as original, but with unpainted headlights	24
012	Anglia Panel	Red body with Malaysia base and chrome hub Whitewall Real Riders	3
N/A	12-Car TH Set	J.C. Penny Box Set, Limited Edition (1 of 3,500)	90

Expected **Average** Cost to acquire the 2002 set car by car, individually (excluding variations): **$55.00**

2003

The most valuable models in the 2003 segment are the red and grey Barracudas. The least valuable model is the Riley & Scott MKIII. Values improved slightly during this release year, but the alternate grey Barracuda blew everything else out of the water. It remains a highly-sought model to this day, and is the 2nd most valuable non-variation TH ever released. 2003 also marked the year HWC.com lowered the production run of the box sets from 3,500 to 1,500...the lowest production number ever released.

Card #	Name	Description	Value
001	Hooligan	White body with purple trim, silver HW logo and chrome hub Real Riders	4
001	Hooligan	Same as original, but with white HW logo	5
002	'56 Ford	Gold body with black Malaysia base and gold hub Real Riders	4
003	Shoe Box	Purple/black body with Malaysia base and chrome hub Whiteline Real Riders	3
004	'68 Cougar	Black body with silver flames and chrome hub Redline Real Riders	5
004	'68 Cougar	Same as original, but with gold flames	8
005	'68 El Camino	Pink/black body with painted headlights and chrome hub Real Riders	4
005	'68 El Camino	Same as original, but with unpainted headlights	5
005	'68 El Camino	Same as original, but "SS" is missing on tailgate	5
006	Porsche 959	Silver body with Malaysia base and chrome hub Real Riders	4
007	Midnight Otto	White body with orange stripes, Malaysia base and chrome hub Real Riders	4
007	Midnight Otto	Same as original, but with red stripes	5
008	Riley & Scott MK	Gold body with blue wing, Malaysia base and chrome hub Real Riders	2
009	'57 Cadillac	Pewter body with Malaysia base and gold/white CoMolds	4
010	Muscle Tone	Black body with Malaysia base and gold hub Real Riders	4
011	Super Tsunami	Antifreeze body with Malaysia base and chrome/grey CoMolds	3
012	Plymouth Cuda	Red/black body with Malaysia base and chrome/grey CoMolds	9
012	Plymouth Cuda	Grey/black body with Malaysia base and chrome/grey CoMolds	157
N/A	12-Car TH Set	HWC.com Box Set, Limited Edition (1 of 1,500)	123

Expected **Average** Cost to acquire the 2003 set car by car, individually (excluding variations): **$50.00**

2004

The most valuable models in the 2004 segment are the Morris Wagon variations. The least valuable model is the Audacious. With the exception of the Morris Wagons, the average values for 2004 TH's were moderate to low.

Card #	Name	Description	Value
101	Pont. Bonneville	Flat lavender body with chrome base and chrome hub Real Rider tires	4
101	Pont. Bonneville	Same as original, but with upside-down HW logo	5
102	GTO-3	Black body with red top, chrome chassis and chrome hub Real Rider tires	4
103	Cadillac Cien	Black body with chrome base and chrome hub Redline Real Rider tires	3
104	The Demon	Gold body with unpainted metal base and chrome hub Whiteline Rear Rider tires	3
104	The Demon	Same as original, but with painted base	8
105	Super Smooth	Metalflake brown and silver body with black base and gold hub Real Rider tires	4
106	Splittin' Image	Pearl white body with unpainted metal base and chrome hub Real Rider tires	3
107	Altered State	Yellow body with black base and chrome hub Real Riders rear/5HSK on front	4
108	Morris Wagon	Gold and black body with metal base and chrome/tan hub Co-Mold wheels	29
108	Morris Wagon	Same as original, but with chrome hub GoodYear Real Riders	33
109	Whip Creamer II	Lime body with chrome base and chrome hub Whiteline Real Rider tires	9
110	Tantrum	Red body with black base and chrome hub Real Rider tires	3
111	Audacious	White body with orange windows 3and chrome hub Real Rider tires	3
012	Meyers Manx	Blue body with metal base and chrome hub Whiteline Real Rider tires	3
N/A	12-Car TH Set	HWC.com Box Set, Limited Edition (1 of 1,500)	100

Expected **Average** Cost to acquire the 2004 set car by car, individually (excluding variations): **$72.00**

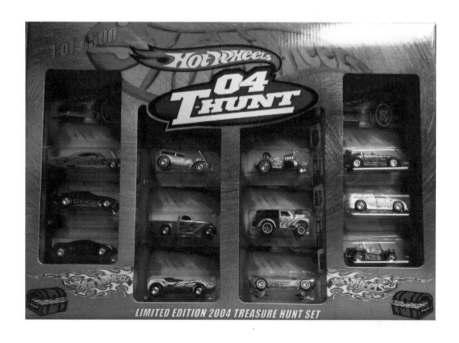

14

2005

Mattel celebrated the 10th Anniversary of Treasure Hunts in style with a special logo, popular castings, and a HUGE bonus: a 13th Treasure Hunt VW Drag Bus. Values for 2005 TH's are generally fair to good, depending on the casting. The ever-popular '67 Camaro was once again a huge hit, and had two major variations: One with a painted motor, and one with Redline Real Riders. The Morris Cooper was also a big mover.

Card #	Name	Description	Value
121	Purple Passion	Black body with flames, chrome chassis and chrome hub Real Rider tires	4
122	'67 Camaro	Red body with unpainted engine and chrome hub Real Rider tires	12
122	'67 Camaro	Same as original, but with painted motor	30
122	'67 Camaro	Same as original, but with Redline Real Riders	85
123	1958 Corvette	Pearl white body with chrome base and Redline chrome hub Real Rider tires	5
123	1958 Corvette	Same as original, but with blackwall Real Riders	7
124	'57 Chevy	Flat black body with metal base and chrome hub Real Rider tires	6
124	'57 Chevy	Same as original, but with painted front grille	6
124	'57 Chevy	Same as original, but with black hub Real Riders	9
125	'56 Flashsider	Black/grey body with unpainted headlights and Whiteline red hub Real Riders	7
125	'56 Flashsider	Same as original, but with painted headlights	10
126	3-Window '34	Brown and grey body with metal base and Whiteline black hub Real Rider tires	4
127	Mustang Mach I	Metalflake blue body with chrome chassis and 5-Spoke Real Rider tires	16
128	'67 Pontiac GTO	Blue body with black roof, chrome base and chrome hub Real Riders	15
129	Rodger Dodger	Black and red body with chrome base and chrome hub Real Rider tires	8
130	Morris Cooper	Yellow body with metal base and chrome lip black hub Real Riders	40
130	Morris Cooper	Same as original, but with no chrome lip on wheels	47
131	'70 Barracuda	Lavender body with chrome base and Whiteline chrome hub Real Riders	8
132	The Demon	Antifreeze body with black roof, metal base and gold hub Real Rider tires	4
133	VW Drag Bus	BONUS. Black with flames, chrome metal base and Redline Real Riders	45
133	VW Drag Bus	Same as original, but with darker base	45
N/A	12-Car TH Set	HWC.com Box Set, Limited Edition (1 of 2,500)	221

Expected **Average** Cost to acquire the 2005 set car by car, individually (excluding variations): **$174.00**

2006

2006 remains a solid year for Treasure Hunt values. The '69 Dodge Charger, with an obvious homage to the General Lee of "Dukes of Hazzard" fame, is the most popular model from this year. It still sells very briskly on the secondary. The '67 Mustang was also a very popular release, as Mustang collectors still shell out decent money for them.

Card #	Name	Description	Value
039	Asphalt Assault	Dark red body with chrome base and chrome 6-Spoke wheels	6
039	Asphalt Assault	Same as original, but with black base	51
040	'40 Ford Coupe	Yellow/black body with chrome base and chrome hub 5-Spoke Real Riders	9
041	Sooo Fast	Copper body with black roof, black base and Redline chrome hub 5-Spoke tires	8
042	Cust. '59 Cadillac	Pearl white body with chrome base and Redline chrome hub Real Rider tires	5
042	Cust. '59 Cadillac	Same as original, but with black interior	30
043	VW New Beetle	White body with black base and orange hub CoMold tires	12
044	'67 Mustang	Pearl white body with metal base and chrome hub 5-Spoke Real Rider tires	17
045	1969 Charger	Orange body with chrome base and chrome hub Real Rider tires	42
045	1969 Charger	Same as original, but with smoked grille	42
046	Hummer H3T	Silver/tan body with unpainted grille and Off-Road chrome hub Real Riders	5
046	Hummer H3T	Same as original, but with black paint on grille and yellow side markers	8
047	CUL8R	Green body with hood stripe, black base and grey hub CoMold 6-Spokes	3
047	CUL8R	Same as original, but missing hood stripe	5
048	C6 Corvette	Black body with black base and gold hub 5-Spoke Real Rider tires	12
049	Pit Cruiser	Purple body with unpainted metal base and 3-Spoke Motorcycle wheels	4
049	Pit Cruiser	Same as original, but with 5-Spoke Motorcycle wheels	12
050	Dairy Delivery	Light green body with gold chrome base and Whiteline gold hub Real Riders	14
N/A	12-Car TH Set	HWC.com Box Set, Limited Edition (1 of 2,000)	164

Expected **Average** Cost to acquire the 2006 set car by car, individually (excluding variations): **$137.00**

2007

2007 marked the year Mattel released Treasure Hunts in a Regular and Super 2-tiered system, where the Deco was the same for both, but the Super paint would be metallic/Spectraflame. Unfortunately, something seems to have occurred in the manufacturing process that caused "flaking" for many of the 2007 models. It's prevalent with the 1969 Camaro Z28, but all models were subject to the problem.

Card #	Name	REGULAR TH's	Value
121	'69 Pontiac GTO	Blue and yellow body with chrome base and 5-Spoke wheels	4
122	Nissan Skyline	Silver/orange/black body with grey base and PR5 wheels	12
123	'69 Camaro Z28	Green body with black roof, chrome base and 5-Spoke wheels	4
124	Corvette C6R	Black body with grey base and gold hub 10-Spoke tires	4
125	Mega Thrust	Orange body with black base and Open Hole 5-Spoke wheels	2
126	Hammer Sled	Yellow body with metal engine/base and 5-Spoke Motorcycle wheels	3
127	Brutalistic	Olive green body with brown metal base and Whitewall 5-Spoke wheels	4
128	Jaded	Metalflake blue body with brown base and 5-Spoke wheels	3
129	Enzo Ferrari	Red body with red seats, black base and PR5 wheels	12
129	Enzo Ferrari	Same as original, but with black seats	27
130	Cust. '69 Chevy	Metalflake gold body with chrome base and PR5 wheels	5
131	Cadillac V16	Pearl red/pink body with chrome base and Open Hole 5-Spoke wheels	3
132	Evil Twin	Metalflake red with chrome base and Open Hole 5-Spoke wheels	3

Card #	Name	$uper TH's (With Spectraflame paint and similar deco as Regulars)	Value
121	'69 Pontiac GTO	Same as original, but with chrome 5-Spoke Real Rider tires	15
122	Nissan Skyline	Spectraflame orange with chrome 6-Spoke Real Rider tires	63
123	'69 Camaro Z28	Spectraflame green with chrome 5-Spoke Real Rider tires	28
123	'69 Camaro Z28	Same as above, but with "T-Hunt" on license plate	42
124	Corvette C6R	Same as original, but with gold 5-Spoke Real Rider tires	18
125	Mega Thrust	Spectraflame orange with chrome 5-Spoke Real Rider tires	8
126	Hammer Sled	Spectraflame antifreeze with yellow hub Real Rider tires	11
127	Brutalistic	Spectraflame olive with chrome 5-Spoke Real Rider tires	8
128	Jaded	Spectraflame blue with chrome 5-Spoke Real Rider tires	10
129	Enzo Ferrari	Spectraflame red with chrome 6-Spoke Real Rider tires	104
130	Cust. '69 Chevy	Spectraflame yellow with chrome 6-Spoke Real Rider tires	15
131	Cadillac V16	Spectraflame red/pink with chrome 6-Spoke whitewall Real Rider tires	15
132	Evil Twin	Spectraflame dark red with chrome 6-Spoke whitewall Real Rider tires	10
N/A	24-Car TH Set	HWC.com Box Set, Limited Edition (1 of 2,000)	300

Expected **Average** Cost to acquire the 2007 set car by car, individually (excluding variations): **$433.00**

2008

The '70 Road Runner was a popular Treasure Hunt in 2008. Both the Regular and $uper versions sell very well on the secondary, while the painted base variation Road Runner is also a highly-sought model.

Card #	Name	REGULAR TH's	Value
161	Chrysler 300 C	Lime and black body with black base and Open-Hole 5-Spoke wheels	3
162	'70 Road Runner	Tan/green and white body with metal base and 5-Spoke wheels	8
163	Rockster	Metalflake green body with chrome base and Off-Road 5-Spoke tires	2
164	Ford Mustang GT	Gold/black body with black base, gold OH5 wheels and 4-stripe tampo	4
164	Ford Mustang GT	Same as original, but with 2-stripe tampo	5
165	Hot Bird	Metalflake gold body with unpainted metal base and 5-Spoke wheels	4
166	Qombee	Metalflake gold body with black roof, black base and PR5 wheels	3
167	Dodge Challenger	Metalflake dark brown body with metal base and 5-Spoke wheels	5
168	Dodge Viper	Orange body with metal base and chrome Open Hole 5-Spoke wheels	3
168	Dodge Viper	Same as original, but with BLACK OH5 wheels	65
169	16 Angels	Dark blue body with metal base and Redline 5-Spoke wheels	2
170	'64 Buick Riviera	Purple body with chrome base and chrome Lace wheels	3
171	Drift King	Black body with black base and chrome Open Hole 5-Spoke wheels	3
172	'69 Camaro	Metalflake grey-blue body with black base and chrome OH5 wheels	5

Card #	Name	$uper TH's (With Spectraflame paint and similar deco as Regulars)	Value
161	Chrysler 300 C	Spectraflame green/flat black with chrome 5-Spoke Real Rider tires	12
162	'70 Road Runner	Spectraflame olive/white with chrome 5-SPoke Real Rider tires	35
162	'70 Road Runner	Same as above, but with painted base	104
163	Rockster	Same as original, but with chrome hub Real Rider tires	7
164	Ford Mustang GT	Spectraflame gold with gold 5-Spoke Real Rider tires	27
165	Hot Bird	Spectraflame gold with chrome 5-Spoke Real Rider tires	25
165	Hot Bird	Same as above, but with painted base	30
166	Qombee	Spectraflame gold with chrome 5-Spoke Real Rider tires	11
167	Dodge Challenger	Spectraflame brown with chrome 5-Spoke Real Rider tires	17
168	Dodge Viper	Spectraflame orange with chrome 5-Spoke Real Rider tires	14
169	16 Angels	Spectraflame dark blue with chrome 5-Spoke Redline Real Rider tires	10
170	'64 Buick Riviera	Spectraflame dark pink with chrome 5-Spoke Real Rider tires	10
171	Drift King	Same as original, but with chrome 5-Spoke Real Rider tires	7
172	'69 Camaro	Spectraflame cyber grey with chrome 5-Spoke Real Rider tires	24
N/A	24-Car TH Set	HWC.com Box Set, Limited Edition (1 of 2,000)	179

Expected **Average** Cost to acquire the 2008 set car by car, individually (excluding variations): **$242.00**

2009

2009 proved to be a very average year for Treasure Hunt vales. Most Regulars can be had for around the $4 range, while only one Super exceeds the $20 threshold (Ford Mustang).

Card #	Name	REGULAR TH's	Value
043	Ford Mustang	Red body with white interior, metal base and 5-Spoke wheels	5
043	Ford Mustang	Same as above, but with painted engine	6
044	'57 Plym. Fury	Metalflake orange body with chrome base and Whiteline 5-Spoke tires	6
045	Bad Bagger	Blue body with metal engine and base, with 3-Spoke Motorcycle tires	4
045	Bad Bagger	Same as above, but on Target "Snowflake" card	13
046	Fire Eater	Red body with chrome base and 5-Spoke wheels	3
047	'37 Ford	Metalflake aqua/brown plastic body with metal base and 5-Spoke wheels	2
048	'34 Ford	Metalflake red and black body with metal base and 5-Spoke wheels	3
049	Cust. '53 Chevy	Metalflake purple body with painted headlights and 5-Spoke wheels	3
049	Cust. '53 Chevy	Same as original, but with unpainted headlights	4
050	Bone Shaker	Gold body with black base, black side tampo and 5-Spoke wheels	4
051	'49 Merc	Metalflake copper body with chrome base and Whitewall 5-Spoke wheels	4
052	'55 Chevy	Metalflake magenta body with unpainted metal base and 5-Spoke wheels	4
053	GMC Motorhome	Grey body with chrome base and orange/black hub OH5 wheels	4
054	Neet Streeter	Metalflake olive body with metal base and 5-Spoke wheels	4

Card #	Name	$uper TH's (With Spectraflame paint and similar deco as Regulars)	Value
043	Ford Mustang	Spectraflame red with chrome hub Redline Real Rider tires	21
044	'57 Plym. Fury	Spectraflame gold with chrome 5-Spoke whiteline Real Rider tires	16
045	Bad Bagger	Spectraflame blue with chrome 5-Spoke Real Rider tires	11
046	Fire Eater	Spectraflame dark red with chrome hub Redline Real Rider tires	13
047	'37 Ford	Spectraflame aqua with red hub whitewall Real Rider tires	13
048	'34 Ford	Metalflake black/red with chrome hub whitewall Real Rider tires	12
049	Cust. '53 Chevy	Spectraflame dark purple with chrome hub whitewall Real Rider tires	12
050	Bone Shaker	Spectraflame gold with chrome 5-Spoke whiteline Real Rider tires	12
051	'49 Merc	Spectraflame brown/tan with chrome hub whitewall Real Rider tires	12
052	'55 Chevy	Spectraflame dark pink with chrome hub whitewall Real Rider tires	18
053	GMC Motorhome	Grey body with chrome hub Redline Real Rider tires	14
054	Neet Streeter	Spectraflame antifreeze with chrome 5-Spoke Real Rider tires	11
N/A	24-Car TH Set	HWC.com Box Set, Limited Edition (1 of 2,000)	197

Expected **Average** Cost to acquire the 2009 set car by car, individually (excluding variations): **$211.00**

2010

Due to their popularity as castings, the Torino, Baja Beetle and Concept Camaro are valued higher than normal Regulars. Only one Super from 2010 is averaging over $20 (#54, Camaro Concept).

Card #	Name	REGULAR TH's	Value
045	'53 Cadillac	Pink body with chrome base and 5-Spoke wheels	3
046	Chevroletor	Red/white body with grey metal base and red/chrome OH5 wheels	2
047	Classic Packard	Metalflake blue body with metal base and chrome Lace wheels	3
048	Ratbomb	Silver body with painted headlights and red outline/ black hub OH5 wheels	2
048	Ratbomb	Same as above, but without painted headlights	3
049	Cobra Daytona	Orange body with chrome base and Open Hole 5-Spoke tires	2
050	Gangster Grin	Metalflake purple body with chrome base and chrome 10-Spoke tires	2
051	Ford GTX-1	Metalflake dark blue body with black base and Open Hole 5-Spoke wheels	2
052	Old Number 5.5	Red body with black base and red chrome 5-Spoke wheels with white tires	2
053	'69 Ford Torino	Green body with black base and black hub 5-Spoke Goodyear tires	6
054	Camaro Concept	Orange body with chrome base and PR5 wheels	5
055	Baja Beetle	Yellow and black body with metal base and Off-Road 5-Spoke wheels	6
056	'69 Ford Mustang	Metalflake light green body and Open-Hole 5-Spoke wheels	4

Card #	Name	$uper TH's (With Spectraflame paint and similar deco as Regulars)	Value
045	'53 Cadillac	Spectraflame magenta with chrome hub whitewall Real Riders	11
046	Chevroletor	Spectraflame red with chrome Star Pro Circuit hubs and Redline Real Riders	9
047	Classic Packard	Spectraflame red with blue hub whitewall Real Riders	11
048	Ratbomb	Metalflake grey with black 5-Spoke Redline Real Riders	9
049	Cobra Daytona	Spectraflame dark orange with chrome 5-Spoke Real Riders	16
050	Gangster Grin	Spectraflame purple with grey Dish hubs and Real Riders	11
051	Ford GTX-1	Spectraflame blue with chrome 5-Spoke Real Riders	12
052	Old Number 5.5	Spectraflame dark red with red 5-Spoke wheels with white Real Riders	15
053	'60 Ford Torino	Spectraflame olive with black hub GoodYear Real Riders	15
054	Camaro Concept	Spectraflame orange with chrome Star Pro Circuit hubs and Real Riders	31
055	Baja Beetle	Spectraflame antifreeze with chrome hub Off-Road Real Riders	17
056	'69 Ford Mustang	Spectraflame green with chrome 5-Spoke Real Riders	16
N/A	24-Car TH Set	HWC.com Box Set, Limited Edition (1 of 2,000)	200

Expected **Average** Cost to acquire the 2010 set car by car, individually (excluding variations): **$186.00**

2011

Mattel increased the number of Regular and $uper TH's to 15 each in 2011. The Datsun 240Z, due to its popularity as a casting, easily remains the most valuable model from 2011.

Card #	Name	Regular TH's	Value
051	Tucker Torpedo	Green body with Malaysia base and black 5-Spoke hubs with whitewall tires	3
052	'57 Chevy	Dark blue body with Goodyear tires with white 5-spoke wheels	4
052	'57 Chevy	Same as above, but with $uper Spectraflame blue paint	10
052	'57 Chevy	Same as original, but with black paint on grille	8
053	'58 Impala	Metalflake lavender body with Malaysia base and 5-Spoke wheels	3
054	Custom '62 Chevy	Metalflake gold body with Malaysia base and PR5 wheels	4
055	Studebaker Avanti	Metalflake gold body with Malaysia base and Whitewall 5-Spoke wheels	4
056	'63 T-Bird	Metalflake green body with Malaysia base and Whitewall 5-Spoke wheels	3
057	'64 Pontiac GTO	Metalflake green body w/orange flame and MC5 wheels	3
057	'64 Pontiac GTO	Same as above, but with painted engine	10
058	'68 Olds 442	Metalflake copper body with Malaysia base and gold/black MC5 wheels	3
059	Corvette G/Sport	Metalflake orange body with Malaysia base and Y5 wheels	3
060	'71 Mustang F/C	Metalflake green body with Malaysia chassis and gold 5-Spoke wheels	4
061	'71 Buick Riviera	Burnt-orange body with white roof, Malaysia base and gold Lace wheels	3
062	Datsun 240Z	White/red body with Malaysia base and chrome/black MC5 wheels	9
063	'80 El Camino	Yellow body with black roof, metal Malaysia base and MC5 wheels	4
064	OCC Splitback	Metalflake copper body with Malaysia base and 3-Spoke M/C wheels	4
065	'59 Chevy	Metalflake blue body with orange flames, Malaysia base and 5-Spoke wheels	4

Card #	Name	$uper TH's (With Spectraflame paint and similar deco as Regulars)	Value
051	Tucker Torpedo	Spectraflame green body with black hub whitewall Real Riders	12
052	'57 Chevy	Spectraflame blue body with white hub Goodyear Real Riders	23
053	'58 Impala	Spectraflame lavender body with chrome hub whitewall Real Riders	15
054	Custom '62 Chevy	Spectraflame lime gold body with Malaysia base and Real Riders	15
055	Studebaker Avanti	Spectraflame gold body with Turbine hubs and whitewall Real Riders	14
056	'63 T-Bird	Spectraflame green body with chrome hub Whitewall Real Riders	11
057	'64 Pontiac GTO	Spectraflame aqua body 5-Spoke Redline Real Riders	13
057	'64 Pontiac GTO	Same as above, but with painted engine	21
058	'68 Olds 442	Spectraflame brown body with chrome slot goldline Real Riders	13
059	Corvette G/Sport	Spectraflame copper body with chrome 10-Spoke Real Riders	15
060	'71 Mustang F/C	Spectraflame green body with gold slot GoodYear Real Riders (rear)	12
061	'71 Buick Riviera	Spectraflame dark red body with white roof and gold 5-Spoke Real Riders	12
062	Datsun 240Z	Spectraflame dark red body with white roof and chrome/black Real Riders	32
063	'80 El Camino	Spectraflame gold with chrome 5-Spoke Real Rider tires	12
064	OCC Splitback	Spectraflame brown body with chrome 3-Spoke MC Real Rider wheels	13
065	'59 Chevy	Spectraflame dark blue body with chrome 5-Spoke Real Riders	12
N/A	30-Car TH Set	HWC.com Box Set, Limited Edition (1 of 2,500)	230

Expected **Average** Cost to acquire the 2011 set car by car, individually (excluding variations): **$282.00**

2012

2012 marked the year that Regulars were completely different castings from $upers. One notable release is the $uper Ferrari 599; its value has skyrocketed to nearly $60. This is likely attributed to the fact that Mattel no longer holds the license to issue Ferrari models. This car also drives up the value of the 2012 Treasure Hunt set.

Card #	Name	Regular TH's	Value
051	'41 WIllys	Metalflake orange body with Malaysia base and MC5 wheels	2
052	Ducati 1098	Yellow body with black seat and black Motorcycle wheels	3
053	'69 Chevelle SS	Metalflake aqua/grey body with red hub GoodYear 5-Spoke wheels	5
054	Ford GT	Red body with black wing, blue windows and chrome PR5 wheels	2
055	'69 Corvette	Metallic blue body with chrome interior and gold/black MC5 wheels	3
056	Tyrrell P34	Red/white body with black hub GoodYear 5-Spoke wheels	3
057	'67 Mustang	Grey/black body with stripe deco and blue/black PR5 wheels	7
058	'52 Chevy	Dark burgundy body with gold roof and black 5-Spoke wheels	5
059	Ferrari 430	Red body with yellow striping and yellow PR5 wheels	6
060	'65 Chevy Malibu	Light metalflake green body with black interior and chrome PR5 wheels	4
061	Ford Shelby GR-1	Yellow body with black interior and yellow/black PR5 wheels	3
062	'65 Ford Ranchero	Light green body with white roof, stripe deco and Lace wheels	3
063	Surf Crate	Lime green body with blue/black Open-Hole 5-Spoke wheels	2
064	'92 Ford Mustang	Aqua body with white roof, stripe and red/black PR5 wheels	6
065	'70 Chevelle	Orange body with black interior, stripe deco and Redline 5-Spoke wheels	4

Card #	Name	$uper TH's (With Spectraflame paint)	Value
084	'69 Dodge Coronet	Spectraflame brown body with chrome/black Real Riders	14
110	'67 Chevelle SS	Spectraflame burgundy body with black hood and black hub Real Riders	14
110	'67 Chevelle SS	Same as above, but with grey interior	15
144	'70 Camaro	Spectraflame burgundy body with star Pro Circuit Real Riders	17
120	Ford Falcon XB	Spectraflame purple body with chrome hub Redline Real Riders	13
120	Ford Falcon XB	Same as above, but with painted headlights	19
082	'71 Challenger	Spectraflame aqua with stripe deco and 5-Spoke Redline Real Riders	18
116	'67 Ford Mustang	Spectraflame gold body with chrome Turbine Redline Real Riders	17
179	'71 Maverick	Spectraflame blue body with white roof, HW Racing deco and Real Riders	11
112	'66 Ford Fairlane	Spectraflame green body black interior and chrome hub Real Riders	12
141	Honda S2000	Spectraflame blue body with "AEM" deco and chrome hub Real Riders	18
125	Ferrari 599	Spectraflame burgundy body with Star Pro Circuit Real Riders	58
108	'69 Camaro Conv.	Spectraflame navy blue body with 5-Spoke Redline Real Riders	14
151	VW Beetle	Spectraflame blue body with white hub 5-Spoke Redline Real Riders	14
132	70 Chevelle Wagon	Spectraflame brown body with gold hub Real Riders	12
129	'09 Ford Focus	Spectraflame burgundy body with chrome hub Redline Real Riders	10
161	'11 Dodge Charger	Spectraflame burgundy body with chrome/red 5-Spoke Real Riders	11

| N/A | 30-Car TH Set | HWC.com Box Set, Limited Edition (1 of 2,000) | 198 |

Expected **Average** Cost to acquire the 2012 set car by car, individually (excluding variations): **$311.00**

2013

2013 saw a drastic drop in popularity for the Regular Treasure Hunts, as values reflected the fact that collectors were regarding them as little more than Mainline issues.

Card #	Name	Regular TH's	Value
041	Bread Box	Pearl white body with "HWPS" deco, chrome interior and 5-Spoke wheels	2
136	Carbonator	Translucent blue body with green base and chrome/blue OH5 wheels	2
017	'10 Camaro SS	Black body with "Police" deco, Malaysia base and red/black PR5 wheels	3
128	Fast Fish	Aqua body with orange base and orange/black PR5 wheels	3
121	Circle Trucker	Green body with 3/Kilpin deco, Malaysia base and yellow/black MC5 wheels	2
036	'64 Lincoln Cont.	Green body with graffiti deco and gold Lace wheels on translucent blue tires	2
051	Sting Rod II	Olive body with orange windows and orange/black 6-Spoke Off-Road wheels	2
101	Prototype H-24	Blue body with HW Racing deco, blue canopy and chrome OH5 wheels	2
101	Prototype H-24	Same as above, but with white/black PR5 wheels	5
032	Custom '77 Van	Black body with yellow windows and green OH5/yellow wheels	2
027	Challenger Drift	White body with black wing chrome/black PR5 wheels	5
014	Mustang Concept	Blue body with Malaysia base and white/black OH5 wheels	2
019	Fire Eater	White body with yellow/red flames, yellow windows and red 5-Spoke wheels	2
092	'12 Ford Fiesta	Red body with racing deco, orange base and white 10-Spoke wheels	2
022	Mazda RX-7	Grey body with black/blue stripe deco, blue interior and PR5 wheels	2
124	Bad To The Blade	Black/orange/aqua body with "8/Hot Wheels" deco and FTE-2 wheels	1

Card #	Name	$uper TH's (With Spectraflame paint)	Value
242	'72 Gran Torino	Spectraflame Aqua body with "K&N" deco and chrome/black Real Riders	12
202	'09 Corvette ZR1	Spectraflame burgundy body and white 10-Spoke Real Riders	15
202	'09 Corvette ZR1	Same as above, but with smoke windows	15
198	'73 Ford Falcon	Spectraflame gold body with chrome/black 5-Spoke Real Riders	12
198	'73 Ford Falcon	Same as above, but with grey interior	18
155	Ford Shelby GT500	Spectraflame green body with gold hub PC5 Real Riders	14
233	'71 El Camino	Spectraflame brown body with gold hub 5-Spoke Real Riders	13
238	'64 Buick Riviera	Purple body with white/black/lavender stripes and chrome hub Real Riders	11
181	Bone Shaker	Spectraflame Pink body with chrome/black hub Real Riders	14
207	'62 Corvette	Spectraflame aqua body with chrome 5-SPoke Real Riders	17
176	Toyota 2000 GT	Spectraflame burgundy body with chrome/black hub Real Riders	14
163	'72 Ford Ranchero	Spectraflame purple body with chrome hub Real Riders	9
197	'69 Camaro	Spectraflame burgundy body with chrome 5-Spoke Real Riders	13
244	'67 Camaro	True Black body with red interior and 5-Spoke Real Riders	23
167	'10 Toyota Tundra	Spectraflame red body with red/black 5-Spoke Off-Road Real Riders	13
229	'07 Ford Mustang	Spectraflame green body with black stripes and chrome 5-Spoke Real Riders	14
229	'07 Ford Mustang	**Signed by Steve Vandervate, Michael Heralda & Phil Riehlman***	NSR
217	'71 Dodge Demon	Spectraflame aqua with chrome/blue 5-Spoke Real Riders	11
N/A	30-Car TH Set	HWC.com Box Set, Limited Edition (1 of 2,000)	178

*This TH is 1 of 12 that were signed and randomly distributed within the line on June 9th, 2013. NSR = No Sales Recorded
Expected **Average** Cost to acquire the 2013 set car by car, individually (excluding variations): **$254.00**

2014

With 2014 Regular Treasure Hunt values falling below the price of shipping on eBay, it makes one wonder if it's truly the best avenue to attain them from! Two pleasant surprises from 2014 are the $uper '55 Bel Air Gasser and the '71 Datsun Bluebird…both of which sell for hefty prices on the secondary.

Card #	Name	Regular TH's	Value
026	Subaru WRX STi	Metalflake silver body with "14" deco, Malaysia base and gold FTE-2 wheels	3
147	Night Burner	Blue body with Hot Wheels racing tampos, Malaysia base and PR5 wheels	1
053	Fangster	Blue/yellow body with orange eyes, yellow base and orange/black OH5 wheels	1
053	Fangster	Same as above, but with translucent smoke tires	2
110	Speedbox	Blue/orange/black body with "Stunt Team" deco and PR5 wheels	2
168	Maximum Leeway	Black body with red interior, Malaysia base and white/black MC5 wheels	1
121	Loop Coupe	Grey body with "Hot Wheels" deco and black 10-spoke hubs on white wheels	1
047	Rescue Duty	Green/white body with yellow windows and red/black hub MC5 wheels	1
177	Stockar	Translucent body with metal base and gold 5-Spoke hubs on translucent tires	2
148	Twinduction	Blue body with HW Racing deco, black base and white PR5 wheels	2
106	'12 Ford Fiesta	White body with Ford/racing deco and red 10-Spoke wheels	2
116	Cust. 71 El Camino	Dark blue body with lined grille and orange/black MC5 wheels	2
116	Cust. 71 El Camino	Same as above, but with no lines on grille	2
184	Off-Track	Green body with yellow windows and 5-spoke hubs/white tires	1
004	Poison Arrow	Translucent red body with yellow trim, blue prop and Micro Wheels	2
034	La Fasta	Light-blue body with smoke windows and gold MC5 wheels	1
077	Cloak & Dagger	Translucent green body with metal base and OH5 wheels	2

Card #	Name	$uper TH's (With Spectraflame paint)	Value
199	Chevrolet SS	Spectraflame blue with black/blue stripes and chrome hub Real Riders	16
202	'13 HW Camaro SE	Spectraflame burgundy with red/black 5-Spoke Real Riders	17
135	Sand Blaster	Spectraflame green with yellow/black 5-Spoke Off-Road Real Riders	12
095	'07 Ford Mustang	Spectraflame red with white stripe deco, tan interior and Real Riders	15
094	71 Mustang Mach I	Spectraflame gold body with orange/black stripes and 5-Spoke Real Riders	18
241	'55 Bel Air Gasser	Spectraflame blue body with "Isky" deco and chrome hub Real Riders	34
243	'70 Chevelle SS	Spectraflame purple body with grey interior and red/black hub Real Riders	11
221	Twin Mill	Spectraflame green body with black stripe and chrome/black hub Real Riders	9
236	'64 Nova Wagon	Spectraflame olive body with flame deco and chrome hub Real Riders	12
136	'83 Chevy Silverado	Spectraflame gold body with stripe deco and chrome/black hub Real Riders	13
237	'76 G/W Corvette	Spectraflame brown body with white/black stripes and tan hub Real Riders	12
214	'69 Corvette	Spectraflame purple body with blue flames and black hub Real Riders	10
218	'65 Chevy Impala	Spectraflame brown body with flame deco and gold hub Real Riders	12
209	Harley Fat Boy	Spectraflame blue body with black seat and 5-Spoke MC Real Riders	13
050	71 Datsun Bluebird	Spectraflame red body with black interior and chrome/black Real Rider wheels	48
050	71 Datsun Bluebird	Same as above, but with smooth front grille	48
N/A	30-Car TH Set	HWC.com Box Set, Limited Edition (1 of 1,000)	259

Expected **Average** Cost to acquire the 2013 set car by car, individually (excluding variations): **$276.00**

the top 25!
Treasure Hunts

We'll give our Treasure Hunts a college feel by compiling a "Top 25" Most Valuable Treasure Hunts issued, through 2014. The list is compiled by dollar value...not popularity. Note that the list is for standard issues only and none of the crazy-valuable variations (next page for those!) As you can see, the rankings are absolutely dominated by the 1995 models...naturally!

Rank	Year	Model	Value
1	1995	'67 Camaro	364.00
2	2003	Plymouth Barracuda (Grey)	157.00
3	1995	VW Bug	125.00
4	2007	Enzo Ferrari	104.00
5	1995	Classic Cobra	82.00
6	1995	'63 Split Window	72.00
7	1995	Olds 442	68.00
8	2007	Nissan Skyline	63.00
9	1995	Gold Passion	63.00
10	1995	Classic Nomad	60.00
11	2012	Ferrari 599	58.00
12	1995	'57 T-Bird	53.00
13	1995	Rolls Royce	50.00
14	2014	'71 Datsun Bluebird	48.00
15	1995	Stutz Blackhawk	48.00
16	2005	VW Drag Bus	45.00
17	1995	'31 Doozie	45.00
18	1995	Classic Caddy	43.00
19	2006	'69 Charger	42.00
20	2005	Morris Cooper	40.00
21	2008	'70 Road Runner	35.00
22	2014	'55 Bel Air Gasser	34.00
23	2011	Datsun 240Z	32.00
24	2010	Chevy Camaro Concept	31.00
25	1996	Lamborghini	30.00

the top 20!
Treasure Hunt Variations

As with all of the Mainline issues, there have been plenty of Treasure Hunt variations over the years. Many of them easily out-value their standard counterparts, and some just go off the charts when it comes to resale value. The following is a list of the Top-20 Most Valuable TH variations. Not surprisingly, the 1995 '67 Camaro variations took the top 2 spots, with the 1995 Gold Passion in a distant 3rd...

Rank	Year	Model	Variation	Value
1	1995	'67 Camaro	Chrome rear wheels	1,142.00
2	1995	'67 Camaro	Missing rear window HW logo	610.00
3	1995	Gold Passion	With pink HW logo	115.00
4	2008	'70 Road Runner	With painted base	104.00
5	2005	'67 Camaro	With Redline Real Riders	85.00
6	1996	'40's Woodie	With gold chrome on rims	80.00
7	1996	Lamborghini	With 5-Spoke wheels	80.00
8	2008	Dodge Viper	With black OH5 wheels	65.00
9	2006	Asphalt Assault	With black base	51.00
10	2014	'71 Datsun Bluebird ($uper)	With smooth grille	48.00
11	2005	Morris Cooper	No chrome on rims	47.00
12	2007	'69 Camaro Z28	With "T-Hunt" on license plate	42.00
13	1999	Ferrari 512M	With 6-Spoke wheels	40.00
14	2000	Pikes Peak Celica	With 3-Spoke wheels	30.00
15	2008	Hot Bird ($uper)	With painted base	30.00
16	2006	Custom '59 Cadillac	With black interior	30.00
17	2005	'67 Camaro	With painted motor	30.00
18	1996	'40's Woodie	With silver on rims	30.00
19	2007	Enzo Ferrari (Regular)	With black seats	27.00
20	1999	Ferrari 512M	With black painted base	26.00

Treasure Hunt Value Comparison Charts

If you're relatively new to collecting TH's, or you're actively filling the holes in your collection, this chart will provide a visual assessment of whether it's beneficial to assemble your TH collection by purchasing the sets, or the cars individually (excluding the valuable variations). As you can see, the results often vary, so you'll have to make a decision on how you want to mix your collection: Box sets, individuals, or a mix of the two? Here's a tip, if you want to go the individual route, but want the box set packaging: You can often find empty TH box sets on eBay to purchase. There's no guarantee you can find the exact year you're looking for, but they do show up from time to time. They're not cheap, either...you'll end up paying a decent amount for the empty packaging. They're fantastically designed, though.

NOTE: I've omitted the 1995 Set/Individual values due to the fact that they're so much more valuable than the ensuing years, they skew the chart's appearance. Check the 1995 Section of this guide to confirm those values.

 = Cost of Treasure Hunt Sets (JC Penny or HWC.com)
= Cost to purchase cars individually

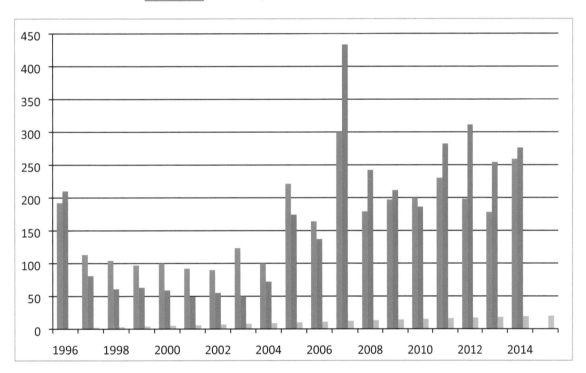

So, how can we interpret these figures? Well, it appears that the Box Sets outweigh the individuals during the early years and vice versa during the later years. This is likely attributed to the fact that collectors went through some lean times with Real Rider-less and uninteresting castings during that period, making the TH Box Sets more appealing.

One more thing to keep in mind, if you're a completist collector: The above values do NOT take into consideration the variations that garner crazy values on the secondary. These will obviously increase your cost of purchasing TH's on an individual basis, if you're so inclined to add them to your set. (The 2003 grey Barracuda comes to mind...)

27

Wheel Chart

There are a multitude of wheels that are used for Treasure Hunts. Below, I've listed a few of the most common, along with the abbreviations used for them throughout the guide. (Some photo credits to Hot Wheels Wiki)

Real Riders

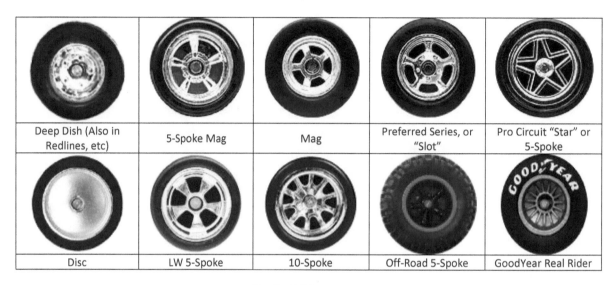

Deep Dish (Also in Redlines, etc)	5-Spoke Mag	Mag	Preferred Series, or "Slot"	Pro Circuit "Star" or 5-Spoke
Disc	LW 5-Spoke	10-Spoke	Off-Road 5-Spoke	GoodYear Real Rider

Non-Real Riders

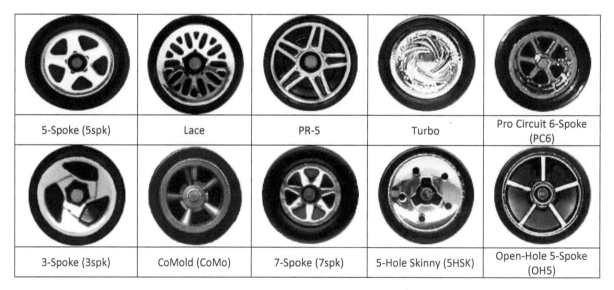

5-Spoke (5spk)	Lace	PR-5	Turbo	Pro Circuit 6-Spoke (PC6)
3-Spoke (3spk)	CoMold (CoMo)	7-Spoke (7spk)	5-Hole Skinny (5HSK)	Open-Hole 5-Spoke (OH5)

Checklists

The following checklists will assist you in cataloguing your collection with the Treasure Hunts that you already have, as well as the ones you're looking to add to your collection. The variations have been listed as well.

Card #	1995 Treasure Hunts	Have It ☺	Want It! ☹
353	Olds 442	☐	☐
354	Gold Passion	☐	☐
354	Gold Passion (Pink HW logo)	☐	☐
355	'67 Camaro	☐	☐
355	'67 Camaro (chrome rear wheels	☐	☐
355	'67 Camaro (No HW logo)	☐	☐
356	'57 T-Bird	☐	☐
357	VW Bug	☐	☐
358	'63 Split Window	☐	☐
359	Stutz Blackhawk	☐	☐
360	Rolls Royce	☐	☐
361	Classic Caddy	☐	☐
362	Classic Nomad	☐	☐
363	Classic Cobra	☐	☐
364	'31 Doozie	☐	☐
N/A	12-Car TH Set	☐	☐

Card #	1996 Treasure Hunts	Have It ☺	Want It! ☹
428	40's Woodie	☐	☐
428	40's Woodie (silver on wheels)	☐	☐
428	40's Woodie (gold on wheels)	☐	☐
429	Lamborghini	☐	☐
429	Lamborghini (5-Spoke wheels)	☐	☐
430	Ferrari 250	☐	☐
431	Jaguar XJ220	☐	☐
432	'59 Caddy	☐	☐
433	Dodge Viper	☐	☐
210	Dodge Viper	☐	☐
434	'57 Chevy	☐	☐
435	Ferrari 355	☐	☐
436	'58 Corvette	☐	☐
437	Auburn 852	☐	☐
438	Dodge Ram	☐	☐
439	'37 Bugatti	☐	☐

Card #	1997 Treasure Hunts	Have It ☺	Want It! ☹
578	'56 Flashsider	☐	☐
579	Silhouette II	☐	☐
580	Mercedes 500SL	☐	☐
581	Street Cleaver	☐	☐
582	GM Lean Machine	☐	☐
583	Hot Rod Wagon	☐	☐
584	Olds Aurora	☐	☐
585	Dogfighter	☐	☐
586	Buick Wildcat	☐	☐
587	Blimp	☐	☐
588	Avus Quattro	☐	☐
589	Rail Rodder	☐	☐
578	'56 Flashsider	☐	☐

Card #	1998 Treasure Hunts	Have It ☺	Want It! ☹
749	Twang Thang	☐	☐
750	Scorchin' Scooter	☐	☐
751	Kenworth T600A	☐	☐
752	3-Window '34	☐	☐
753	Turbo Flame	☐	☐
754	Saltflat Racer	☐	☐
755	Street Beast	☐	☐
756	Road Rocket	☐	☐
757	Sol-Aire CX7	☐	☐
758	'57 Chevy	☐	☐
759	Stingray III	☐	☐
760	Way 2 Fast	☐	☐
749	Twang Thang	☐	☐

Card #	1999 Treasure Hunts	Have It ☺	Want It! ☹
929	Mercedes 540K	☐	☐
930	T-Bird Stocker	☐	☐
931	'97 Corvette	☐	☐
932	Rigor Motor	☐	☐
933	Ferrari 512M	☐	☐
933	Ferrari 512M (painted base)	☐	☐
933	Ferrari 512M (6-Spoke wheels)	☐	☐
934	'59 Impala	☐	☐
935	Hot Wheels 500	☐	☐
936	Jaguar D-Type	☐	☐
937	'32 Ford Delivery	☐	☐
938	Hot Seat	☐	☐
939	Mustang Mach I	☐	☐
940	Express Lane	☐	☐

Card #	2000 Treasure Hunts	Have It ☺	Want It! ☹
49	Double Vision	☐	☐
50	Tow Jam	☐	☐
51	1936 Cord	☐	☐
51	1936 Cord (Whitewalls)	☐	☐
52	Sweet 16 II	☐	☐
53	Lakester	☐	☐
54	Go Kart	☐	☐
55	Chaparral II	☐	☐
56	'57 T-Bird	☐	☐
57	Pikes Peak Celica (Gold RR's)	☐	☐
57	Pikes Peak Celica (Chrome RR's)	☐	☐
57	Pikes Peak Celica (3-Spoke wheels)	☐	☐
58	'67 Pontiac GTO	☐	☐
58	'67 Pontiac GTO (Thailand base)	☐	☐
59	Ford GT-40	☐	☐
60	1970 Chevelle	☐	☐

Card #	2001 Treasure Hunts	Have It ☺	Want It! ☹
001	'65 Corvette	☐	☐
002	Roll Cage	☐	☐
003	So Fine	☐	☐
004	Rodger Dodger	☐	☐
005	Blast Lane	☐	☐
006	Hammered Coupe	☐	☐
007	Vulture	☐	☐
008	'67 Charger	☐	☐
009	Olds 442	☐	☐
010	Pontiac Rageous	☐	☐
011	Deora	☐	☐
012	Cabbin' Fever	☐	☐

Card #	2002 Treasure Hunts	Have It ☺	Want It! ☹
001	La Troca	☐	☐
002	Plymouth GTX	☐	☐
003	'57 Roadster	☐	☐
003	'57 Roadster (All 5spk wheels)	☐	☐
004	Lotus M250	☐	☐
005	Ford Thunderbolt	☐	☐
006	Panoz LMP-1	☐	☐
007	Phaeton	☐	☐
008	F/Fendered '40	☐	☐
008	F/Fendered '40 (semi-gloss black)	☐	☐
009	'40 Ford Truck	☐	☐
010	Tail Dragger	☐	☐
011	Mini Cooper	☐	☐
011	Mini Cooper (no headlight paint)	☐	☐
012	Anglia Panel	☐	☐

Card #	2003 Treasure Hunts	Have It ☺	Want It! ☹
001	Hooligan	☐	☐
001	Hooligan (white HW logo)	☐	☐
002	'56 Ford	☐	☐
003	Shoe Box	☐	☐
004	'68 Cougar	☐	☐
004	'68 Cougar (gold flames)	☐	☐
005	'68 El Camino	☐	☐
005	'68 El Camino (no headlight paint)	☐	☐
005	'68 El Camino ("SS" missing)	☐	☐
006	Porsche 959	☐	☐
007	Midnight Otto	☐	☐
007	Midnight Otto (with red stripes)	☐	☐
008	Riley & Scott MK	☐	☐
009	'57 Cadillac	☐	☐
010	Muscle Tone	☐	☐
011	Super Tsunami	☐	☐
012	Plymouth Cuda (Red/black)	☐	☐
012	Plymouth Cuda (Grey/black)	☐	☐

Card #	2004 Treasure Hunts	Have It ☺	Want It! ☹
001	Hooligan	☐	☐
001	Hooligan (white HW logo)	☐	☐
002	'56 Ford	☐	☐
003	Shoe Box	☐	☐
004	'68 Cougar	☐	☐
004	'68 Cougar (gold flames)	☐	☐
005	'68 El Camino	☐	☐
005	'68 El Camino (no headlight paint)	☐	☐
005	'68 El Camino ("SS" missing)	☐	☐
006	Porsche 959	☐	☐
007	Midnight Otto	☐	☐
007	Midnight Otto (with red stripes)	☐	☐
008	Riley & Scott MK	☐	☐
009	'57 Cadillac	☐	☐
010	Muscle Tone	☐	☐
011	Super Tsunami	☐	☐
012	Plymouth Cuda (Red/black)	☐	☐
012	Plymouth Cuda (Grey/black)	☐	☐

Card #	2005 Treasure Hunts	Have It ☺	Want It! ☹
121	Purple Passion	☐	☐
122	'67 Camaro	☐	☐
122	'67 Camaro (painted motor)	☐	☐
122	'67 Camaro (Redline RR's)	☐	☐
123	1958 Corvette	☐	☐
123	1958 Corvette (Blackwall RR's)	☐	☐
124	'57 Chevy	☐	☐
124	'57 Chevy (painted grille)	☐	☐
124	'57 Chevy (Black hub RR's)	☐	☐
125	'56 Flashsider	☐	☐
125	'56 Flashsider (painted headlights)	☐	☐
126	3-Window '34	☐	☐
127	Mustang Mach I	☐	☐
128	'67 Pontiac GTO	☐	☐
129	Rodger Dodger	☐	☐
130	Morris Cooper	☐	☐
130	Morris Cooper (no wheel chrome)	☐	☐
131	'70 Barracuda	☐	☐
132	The Demon	☐	☐
133	VW Drag Bus	☐	☐
133	VW Drag Bus (dark base)	☐	☐

Card #	2006 Treasure Hunts	Have It ☺	Want It! ☹
039	Asphalt Assault	☐	☐
039	Asphalt Assault (black base)	☐	☐
040	'40 Ford Coupe	☐	☐
041	Sooo Fast	☐	☐
042	Cust. '59 Cadillac	☐	☐
042	Cust. '59 Cadillac (black interior)	☐	☐
043	VW New Beetle	☐	☐
044	'67 Mustang	☐	☐
045	1969 Charger	☐	☐
045	1969 Charger (smoke grille)	☐	☐
046	Hummer H3T	☐	☐
046	Hummer H3T (painted grille)	☐	☐
047	CUL8R	☐	☐
047	CUL8R (missing hood stripe)	☐	☐
048	C6 Corvette	☐	☐
049	Pit Cruiser	☐	☐
049	Pit Cruiser (with 5spk MC wheels)	☐	☐
050	Dairy Delivery	☐	☐

Card #	2007 Regular Treasure Hunts	Have It ☺	Want It! ☹
121	'69 Pontiac GTO	☐	☐
122	Nissan Skyline	☐	☐
123	'69 Camaro Z28	☐	☐
124	Corvette C6R	☐	☐
125	Mega Thrust	☐	☐
126	Hammer Sled	☐	☐
127	Brutalistic	☐	☐
128	Jaded	☐	☐
129	Enzo Ferrari	☐	☐
129	Enzo Ferrari (black seats)	☐	☐
130	Cust. '69 Chevy	☐	☐
131	Cadillac V16	☐	☐
132	Evil Twin	☐	☐

Card #	2007 $uper Treasure Hunts	Have It ☺	Want It! ☹
121	'69 Pontiac GTO	☐	☐
122	Nissan Skyline	☐	☐
123	'69 Camaro Z28	☐	☐
123	'69 Camaro Z28 ("T-Hunt on plate)	☐	☐
124	Corvette C6R	☐	☐
125	Mega Thrust	☐	☐
126	Hammer Sled	☐	☐
127	Brutalistic	☐	☐
128	Jaded	☐	☐
129	Enzo Ferrari	☐	☐
130	Cust. '69 Chevy	☐	☐
131	Cadillac V16	☐	☐
132	Evil Twin	☐	☐

Card #	2008 Regular Treasure Hunts	Have It ☺	Want It! ☹
161	Chrysler 300 C	☐	☐
162	'70 Road Runner	☐	☐
163	Rockster	☐	☐
164	Ford Mustang GT (4 stripes)	☐	☐
164	Ford Mustang GT (2 stripes)	☐	☐
165	Hot Bird	☐	☐
166	Qombee	☐	☐
167	Dodge Challenger	☐	☐
168	Dodge Viper	☐	☐
168	Dodge Viper (black OH5 wheels)	☐	☐
169	16 Angels	☐	☐
170	'64 Buick Riviera	☐	☐
171	Drift King	☐	☐
172	'69 Camaro	☐	☐

Card #	2008 $uperTreasure Hunts	Have It ☺	Want It! ☹
161	Chrysler 300 C	☐	☐
162	'70 Road Runner	☐	☐
162	'70 Road Runner (painted base)	☐	☐
163	Rockster	☐	☐
164	Ford Mustang GT	☐	☐
165	Hot Bird	☐	☐
165	Hot Bird (painted base)	☐	☐
166	Qombee	☐	☐
167	Dodge Challenger	☐	☐
168	Dodge Viper	☐	☐
169	16 Angels	☐	☐
170	'64 Buick Riviera	☐	☐
171	Drift King	☐	☐
172	'69 Camaro	☐	☐

Card #	2009 Regular Treasure Hunts	Have It ☺	Want It! ☹
043	Ford Mustang	☐	☐
043	Ford Mustang (painted motor)	☐	☐
044	'57 Plym. Fury	☐	☐
045	Bad Bagger	☐	☐
045	Bad Bagger (Snowflake card)	☐	☐
046	Fire Eater	☐	☐
047	'37 Ford	☐	☐
048	'34 Ford	☐	☐
049	Cust. '53 Chevy	☐	☐
049	Cust. '53 Chevy (unpainted lights)	☐	☐
050	Bone Shaker	☐	☐
051	'49 Merc	☐	☐
052	'55 Chevy	☐	☐
053	GMC Motorhome	☐	☐
054	Neet Streeter	☐	☐

Card #	2009 $uper Treasure Hunts	Have It ☺	Want It! ☹
043	Ford Mustang	☐	☐
044	'57 Plym. Fury	☐	☐
045	Bad Bagger	☐	☐
046	Fire Eater	☐	☐
047	'37 Ford	☐	☐
048	'34 Ford	☐	☐
049	Cust. '53 Chevy	☐	☐
050	Bone Shaker	☐	☐
051	'49 Merc	☐	☐
052	'55 Chevy	☐	☐
053	GMC Motorhome	☐	☐
054	Neet Streeter	☐	☐

Card #	2010 Regular Treasure Hunts	Have It ☺	Want It! ☹
045	'53 Cadillac	☐	☐
046	Chevroletor	☐	☐
047	Classic Packard	☐	☐
048	Ratbomb	☐	☐
048	Ratbomb (no painted lights)	☐	☐
049	Cobra Daytona	☐	☐
050	Gangster Grin	☐	☐
051	Ford GTX-1	☐	☐
052	Old Number 5.5	☐	☐
053	'69 Ford Torino	☐	☐
054	Camaro Concept	☐	☐
055	Baja Beetle	☐	☐
056	'69 Ford Mustang	☐	☐

Card #	2010 $uper Treasure Hunts	Have It ☺	Want It! ☹
045	'53 Cadillac	☐	☐
046	Chevroletor	☐	☐
047	Classic Packard	☐	☐
048	Ratbomb	☐	☐
049	Cobra Daytona	☐	☐
050	Gangster Grin	☐	☐
051	Ford GTX-1	☐	☐
052	Old Number 5.5	☐	☐
053	'60 Ford Torino	☐	☐
054	Camaro Concept	☐	☐
055	Baja Beetle	☐	☐
056	'69 Ford Mustang	☐	☐

Card #	2011 Regular Treasure Hunts	Have It ☺	Want It! ☹
051	Tucker Torpedo	☐	☐
052	'57 Chevy	☐	☐
052	'57 Chevy (Spectraflame paint)	☐	☐
052	'57 Chevy (black painted grille)	☐	☐
053	'58 Impala	☐	☐
054	Custom '62 Chevy	☐	☐
055	Studebaker Avanti	☐	☐
056	'63 T-Bird	☐	☐
057	'64 Pontiac GTO	☐	☐
057	'64 Pontiac GTO (painted motor)	☐	☐
058	'68 Olds 442	☐	☐
059	Corvette G/Sport	☐	☐
060	'71 Mustang F/C	☐	☐
061	'71 Buick Riviera	☐	☐
062	Datsun 240Z	☐	☐
063	'80 El Camino	☐	☐
064	OCC Splitback	☐	☐
065	'59 Chevy	☐	☐

Card #	2011 $uper Treasure Hunts	Have It ☺	Want It! ☹
051	Tucker Torpedo	☐	☐
052	'57 Chevy	☐	☐
053	'58 Impala	☐	☐
054	Custom '62 Chevy	☐	☐
055	Studebaker Avanti	☐	☐
056	'63 T-Bird	☐	☐
057	'64 Pontiac GTO	☐	☐
057	'64 Pontiac GTO (painted motor)	☐	☐
058	'68 Olds 442	☐	☐
059	Corvette G/Sport	☐	☐
060	'71 Mustang F/C	☐	☐
061	'71 Buick Riviera	☐	☐
062	Datsun 240Z	☐	☐
063	'80 El Camino	☐	☐
064	OCC Splitback	☐	☐
065	'59 Chevy	☐	☐

Card #	2012 Regular Treasure Hunts	Have It ☺	Want It! ☹
051	'41 WIllys	☐	☐
052	Ducati 1098	☐	☐
053	'69 Chevelle SS	☐	☐
054	Ford GT	☐	☐
055	'69 Corvette	☐	☐
056	Tyrrell P34	☐	☐
057	'67 Mustang	☐	☐
058	'52 Chevy	☐	☐
059	Ferrari 430	☐	☐
060	'65 Chevy Malibu	☐	☐
061	Ford Shelby GR-1	☐	☐
062	'65 Ford Ranchero	☐	☐
063	Surf Crate	☐	☐
064	'92 Ford Mustang	☐	☐
065	'70 Chevelle	☐	☐

Card #	2012 $uper Treasure Hunts	Have It ☺	Want It! ☹
084	'69 Dodge Coronet	☐	☐
110	'67 Chevelle SS	☐	☐
110	'67 Chevelle SS (grey interior)	☐	☐
144	'70 Camaro	☐	☐
120	Ford Falcon XB	☐	☐
120	Ford Falcon XB (painted lights)	☐	☐
082	'71 Challenger	☐	☐
116	'67 Ford Mustang	☐	☐
179	'71 Maverick	☐	☐
112	'66 Ford Fairlane	☐	☐
141	Honda S2000	☐	☐
125	Ferrari 599	☐	☐
108	'69 Camaro Conv.	☐	☐
151	VW Beetle	☐	☐
2	70 Chevelle Wagon	☐	☐
129	'09 Ford Focus	☐	☐
161	'11 Dodge Charger	☐	☐

Card #	2013 Regular Treasure Hunts	Have It ☺	Want It! ☹
041	Bread Box	☐	☐
136	Carbonator	☐	☐
017	'10 Camaro SS	☐	☐
128	Fast Fish	☐	☐
121	Circle Trucker	☐	☐
036	'64 Lincoln Cont.	☐	☐
051	Sting Rod II	☐	☐
101	Prototype H-24	☐	☐
101	Prototype H-24 (white/black PR5's)	☐	☐
032	Custom '77 Van	☐	☐
027	Challenger Drift	☐	☐
014	Mustang Concept	☐	☐
019	Fire Eater	☐	☐
092	'12 Ford Fiesta	☐	☐
022	Mazda RX-7	☐	☐
124	Bad To The Blade	☐	☐

Card #	2013 $uper Treasure Hunts	Have It ☺	Want It! ☹
242	'72 Gran Torino	☐	☐
202	'09 Corvette ZR1	☐	☐
202	'09 Corvette ZR1 (smoke windows)	☐	☐
198	'73 Ford Falcon	☐	☐
198	'73 Ford Falcon (grey interior)	☐	☐
155	Ford Shelby GT500	☐	☐
233	'71 El Camino	☐	☐
238	'64 Buick Riviera	☐	☐
181	Bone Shaker	☐	☐
207	'62 Corvette	☐	☐
176	Toyota 2000 GT	☐	☐
163	'72 Ford Ranchero	☐	☐
197	'69 Camaro	☐	☐
244	'67 Camaro	☐	☐
167	'10 Toyota Tundra	☐	☐
229	'07 Ford Mustang	☐	☐
229	'07 Ford Mustang (autographed)	☐	☐
217	'71 Dodge Demon	☐	☐

Card #	2014 Regular Treasure Hunts	Have It ☺	Want It! ☹
026	Subaru WRX STi	☐	☐
147	Night Burner	☐	☐
053	Fangster	☐	☐
053	Fangster (translucent tires)	☐	☐
110	Speedbox	☐	☐
168	Maximum Leeway	☐	☐
121	Loop Coupe	☐	☐
047	Rescue Duty	☐	☐
177	Stockar	☐	☐
148	Twinduction	☐	☐
106	'12 Ford Fiesta	☐	☐
116	Cust. 71 El Camino	☐	☐
116	Cust. 71 El Camino (no grille lines)	☐	☐
184	Off-Track	☐	☐
004	Poison Arrow	☐	☐
034	La Fasta	☐	☐
077	Cloak & Dagger	☐	☐

Card #	2014 $uper Treasure Hunts	Have It ☺	Want It! ☹
199	Chevrolet SS	☐	☐
202	'13 HW Camaro SE	☐	☐
135	Sand Blaster	☐	☐
095	'07 Ford Mustang	☐	☐
094	71 Mustang Mach I	☐	☐
241	'55 Bel Air Gasser	☐	☐
243	'70 Chevelle SS	☐	☐
221	Twin Mill	☐	☐
236	'64 Nova Wagon	☐	☐
136	'83 Chevy Silverado	☐	☐
237	'76 G/W Corvette	☐	☐
214	'69 Corvette	☐	☐
218	'65 Chevy Impala	☐	☐
209	Harley Fat Boy	☐	☐
050	71 Datsun Bluebird	☐	☐
050	71 Datsun Bluebird (smooth grille)	☐	☐

GALLERY

To close out the Hot Wheels Treasure Hunt Price Guide, we'll take a look at some outstanding photography of Hot Wheels Treasure Hunts. Photo credits can be found under each model.

2013 Chevy Camaro SE (Photo Credit Tony Szuta)

'62 Corvette (Photo Credit Tony Szuta)

Chevy Camaro Concept (Photo Credit Tony Szuta)

Ferrari 599XX (Photo Credit Tony Szuta)

Custom '07 Ford Mustang (Photo Credit hwcollectorsnews.com)

Chevrolet SS (Photo Credit healnot/Wiki)

Toyota 2000GT (Photo Credit, Lamley Group

Nissan Skyline (Photo Credit, Wikia)

Chevelle SS (Photo Credit Wikia)

55 Chevy Bel Air Gasser (Photo Credit Wikia)

about the author

Neal Giordano is a Rhode Island native who was transplanted to North Carolina in 1987, when he checked in to the Marine Corps Air Station at Cherry Point after graduating from Marine boot camp in Parris Island, South Carolina.

After serving in Operations Desert Shield and Desert Storm, he completed his Marine Corps enlistment in 1991, and was married in 1992, resulting in his pride and joy of 3 kids: Carson, Cherie and Anthony. Today, he is currently resides in Apex, and is a Security Manager for a Fortune 500 company in Cary, North Carolina. He is also an avid Redline, Blackwall and vintage Matchbox collector.

Neal is the founder/editor of the North Carolina Hot Wheels Association website, which is one of the older Hot Wheels websites on the Internet. In his own words on the hobby:

"As the boys grew older, we were able to buy WAY cooler toys that piqued my interest as well. Hot Wheels were definitely something they enjoyed, and that triggered a lot of amazing memories that I had of playing with Hot Wheels and Matchbox cars as a kid."

"I missed out on the Redline era for the most part, catching only the last couple of years before the red stripes were removed from the tires. So, technically, I grew up in the Blackwall era…but, it was still a blast. We ran those cars through mud, water and who knows what else. They saw very little "track time." My parents bought me my first Hot Wheels set in 1975: the Thundershift 500. I must've logged a thousand hours on that track."

"Years later, around 1995 or so, I'm buying Hot Wheels for my boys, which got me thinking: this could be a really cool, inexpensive (don't laugh…I was completely naïve at the time!) hobby. So, I got back into Hot Wheels as an adult. Three years later, I started the North Carolina Hot Wheels Association website on Geocities, and it kept growing…and growing. It's now a massive database of Hot Wheels, from Redlines to present. It also includes vintage Lesney Matchbox guides, from the 50's through the 90's, as well as a Corgi guide."

"In the early days, the website eventually led to 7 collectors getting together in a K*Mart parking lot in Raleigh on a frigid February day in the waning days of Winter, 1998. We held a Trunk Trade, and braved the cold wind…but, everyone still enjoyed themselves. Word began to spread, and those 7 collectors eventually turned into a huge group that included collectors in Texas, South Carolina, Virginia, New Jersey and other states. We began to put on Trade Shows, where collectors could meet, buy, sell and trade. Shortly after, a few amazing members constructed an incredible downhill track, complete with 4 lanes and a digital finish line." Before we knew it, we were hosting Mattel Hot Wheels designers, and holding shows in malls that attracted collectors from all over. It was the best!"

"Now, all these years later, the club has long since been inactive, having been so since 2003. After a 5 year break from the website, I picked up the NCHWA.com URL again in 2008, and continued what I started back in 1998."

"This publication is for all Hot Wheels collectors, young and young at heart. I'd like to personally thank all of the visitors who support NCHWA.com; you're the reason I continue to try and offer a solid resource for Hot Wheels, Matchbox and Corgi collectors. I hope this Treasure Hunt guide helps you with your hobby."

Neal Giordano can be reached via email at nchwa@yahoo.com – I'm always available to answer questions!
You can also interact with us through the NCHWA Facebook page at www.facebook.com/NCHWA

07 Ford Mustang (23)
07 Ford Mustang (24)
09 Corvette ZR1 (23)
09 Ford Focus
10 Camaro SS (23)
10 Toyota Tundra (23)
11 Dodge Charger
12 Ford Fiesta (23)
12 Ford Fiesta (24)
13 HW Camaro SE (24)
16 Angels (18)
1936 Cord (10)
1958 Corvette (15)
1969 Charger (16)
1970 Chevelle (10)
31 Doozie (5)
32 Ford Delivery (9)
34 Ford (19)
37 Bugatti (6)
37 Ford (19)
3-Window 34 (15)
3-Window 34 (8)
40 Ford Coupe (16)
40 Ford Truck (12)
40's Woodie (6)
41 Willys (22)
49 Merc (19)
52 Chevy (22)
53 Cadillac (20)
55 Bel Air Gasser (24)
55 Chevy (19)
56 Flashsider (15)
56 Flashsider (7)
56 Ford (13)
57 Cadillac (13)
57 Chevy (15)
57 Chevy (21)
57 Chevy (6)
57 Chevy (8)
57 Plymouth Fury (19)

57 Roadster (12)
57 T-Bird (10)
57 T-Bird (5)
58 Corvette (6)
58 Impala (21)
59 Chevy (21)
59 Impala (9)
62 Corvette (23)
63 Split Window (5)
63 T-Bird (21)
64 Buick Riviera (18)
64 Buick Riviera (23)
64 Linc. Continental (23)
64 Nova Wagon (24)
64 Pontiac GTO (21)
65 Chevy Impala (24)
65 Chevy Malibu (22)
65 Corvette (11)
65 Ford Ranchero (22)
66 Ford Fairlane (22)
67 Camaro (15)
67 Camaro (5)
67 Charger (11)
67 Chevelle SS (22)
67 Ford Mustang (22)
67 Mustang (16)
67 Mustang (22)
67 Pontiac GTO (10)
67 Pontiac GTO (15)
68 Cougar (13)
68 El Camino (13)
68 Olds 442 (21)
69 Camaro (18)
69 Camaro (23)
69 Camaro Convert. (22)
69 Camaro Z28 (17)
69 Chevelle SS (22)
69 Corvette (22)
69 Corvette (24)
69 Dodge Coronet (22)

69 Ford Mustang (20)
69 Ford Torino (20)
69 Pontiac GTO (17)
70 Barracuda (15)
70 Camaro (22)
70 Chevelle (22)
70 Chevelle SS (24)
70 Chevelle Wagon (22)
70 Road Runner (18)
71 Buick Riviera (21)
71 Challenger (22)
71 Datsun Bluebird (24)
71 Dodge Demon (23)
71 El Camino (23)
71 Maveric Grabber (22)
71 Mustang Funny Car (21)
71 Mustang Mach I (24)
72 Ford Ranchero (23)
72 Gran Torino (23)
73 Ford Falcon
76 G/W Corvette (24)
80 El Camino (21)
83 Chevy Silverado (24)
92 Ford Mustang (22)
97 Corvette (9)
Altered State (14)
Anglia Panel (12)
Asphault Assault (16)
Auburn 852 (6)
Audacious (14)
Avus Quattro (7)
Bad Bagger (19)
Bad to the Blade (23)
Baja Beetle (20)
Blast Lane (11)
Blimp (7)
Bone Shaker (19)
Bone Shaker (23)
Bread Box (23)
Brutalistic (17)

Buick Wildcat (7)

Fangster (24)

Lamborghini (6)

C6 Corvette (16)	Fast Fish (23)	Loop Coupe (24)
Cabbin' Fever (11)	Fat Fendered 40 (12)	Lotus M250 (12)
Cadillac Cien (14)	Ferrari 250 (6)	Maximum Leeway (24)
Cadillac V16 (17)	Ferrari 35 (6)	Mazda RX-7 (23)
Camaro Concept (20)	Ferrari 430 (22)	Mega Thrust (17)
Carbonator (23)	Ferrari 512M (9)	Mercedes 500SL (7)
Challenger Drift (23)	Ferrari 599 (22)	Mercedes 540K (9)
Chaparral II (10)	Fire Eater (19)	Meyers Manx (14)
Chevrolet SS (24)	Fire Eater (23)	Midnight Otto (13)
Chevroletor (20)	Ford Falcon XB (22)	Mini Cooper (12)
Chrysler 300C (18)	Ford GT (22)	Morris Cooper (15)
Circle Trucker (23)	Ford GT-40 (10)	Morris Wagon (14)
Classic Caddy (5)	Ford GTX-1 (20)	Muscle Tone (13)
Classic Cobra (5)	Ford Mustang (19)	Mustang Concept (23)
Classic Nomad (5)	Ford Mustang GT (18)	Mustang Mach I (15)
Classic Packard (20)	Ford Shelby GR-1 (22)	Mustang Mach I (9)
Cloack & Dagger (24)	Ford Shelby GT500 (23)	Neet Streeter (19)
Corvette C6R (17)	Ford Thunderbolt (12)	Night Burner (24)
Corvette G/Sport (21)	Gangster Grin (20)	Nissan Skyline (17)
CUL8R (16)	GM Lean Machine (7)	OCC Splitback (21)
Cust. 71 El Camino (24)	GMC Motorhome (19)	Off-Track (24)
Custom 53 Chevy (19)	Go Kart (10)	Old Number 5.5 (20)
Custom 59 Cadillac (16)	Gold Passion (5)	Olds 442 (11)
Custom 62 Chevy (21)	GTO-3 (14)	Olds 442 (5)
Custom 69 Chevy (17)	Hammer Sled (17)	Olds Aurora (7)
Custom 77 Van (23)	Hammered Coupe (11)	Panoz LMP-1 (12)
Dairy Delivery (16)	Harley Davidson (24)	Phaeton (12)
Datsun 240Z (21)	Honda S2000 (22)	Pikes Peak Celica (10)
Deora (11)	Hooligan (13)	Pit Cruiser (16)
Dodge Challenger (18)	Hot Bird (18)	Plymouth Cuda (13)
Dodge Ram (6)	Hot Rod Wagon (7)	Plymouth GTX (12)
Dodge Viper (18)	Hot Seat (9)	Poison Arrow (24)
Dodge Viper (6)	Hot Wheels 500 (9)	Pontiac Bonneville (14)
Dogfighter (7)	Hummer H3T (16)	Pontiac Rageous (11)
Double Vision (10)	Jaded (17)	Porsche 959 (13)
Drift King (18)	Jaguar D-Type (9)	Protoype H-24 (23)
Ducati 1098 (22)	Jaguar XJ220 (6)	Purple Passion (15)
Enzo Ferrari (17)	Kenworth T600A (8)	Qombee (18)
Evil Twin (17)	La Fasta (24)	Rail Rodder (7)
Express Lane (9)	La Troca (12)	Ratbomb (20)
	Lakester (10)	Rescue Duty (24)

Rigor Motor (9)

Riley & Scott MK (13)

Road Rocket (8)

Rockster (18)

Rodger Dodger (11)

Rodger Dodger (15)

Roll Cage (11)

Rolls Royce (5)

Saltflat Racer (8)

Sand Blaster (24)

Scorchin' Scooter (8)

Shelby Cobra Daytona (20)

Shoe Box (13)

Silhouette II (7)

So Fine (11)

Sol-Aire CX7 (8)

Sooo Fast (16)

Speedbox (24)

Splittin' Image (14)

Sting Rod II (23)

Stingray III (8)

Stockar (24)

Street Beast (8)

Street Cleaver (7)

Studebaker Avanti (21)

Stutz Blackhawk (5)

Subaru WRX Sti (24)

Super Smooth (14)

Super Tsunami (13)

Surf Crate (22)

Sweet 16 II (10)

Tail Dragger (12)

Tantrum (14)

T-Bird Stocker (9)

The Demon (14)

The Demon (15)

Tow Jam (10)

Toyota 2000 GT (23)

Tucker Torpedo (21)

Turbo Flame (8)

Twang Thang (8)

Twin Mill (24)

Twinduction (24)

Tyrrell P34 (22)

Vulture (11)

VW Beetle (22)

VW Bug (5)

VW Drag Bus (15)

VW New Beetle (16)

Way 2 Fast (8)

Whip Creamer II (14)

Printed in the USA
CPSIA information can be obtained
at www.ICGtesting.com
LVHW072103031023
760054LV00002B/4